The Low Country

TEXT AND ILLUSTRATIONS BY
MALLORY PEARCE
FOREWORD BY JANISSE RAY

MAUDLIN POND PRESS
2021

© 2010 by Mallory Pearce
ISBN 978-0-615-41413-3
Printed and bound in the United States of America
Maudlin Pond Press
P. O. Box 53
Tybee Island, GA 31522
www.maudlinpond.com

Many of the illustrations came from the following
books by Mallory Pearce:
Seashore Life Illustrations
© 1999 by Dover Publications, Inc.
Wetlands Plants and Animals
© 2003 by Dover Publications, Inc.
Forest Plants and Animals Illustrations
© 2005 by Dover Publications, Inc.
Used with permission.

The Low Country

FOREWORD
By Janisse Ray

Equal to the power of a human over a landscape is the power a landscape wields over a human. A person can be transformed by land. That is what happened in 1950 when a teenage boy from upstate New York moved to Tybee Island and came of age among the briny marshes and salty beaches of coastal Georgia. The boy was captivated wholly and changed forever.

"Perhaps atoms merge out of the landscape into us," wrote Ivan Doig.

For Tybee Island to mold Mallory Pearce into a naturalist is no great wonder to me. Some of the most beautiful sights I have seen in nature I saw in the labyrinthine salt creeks that flood and drain the spartina flats of this spectacular place – a doe swimming South Cut, flying fish, pods of dolphin, a stingray on the tip of my fishing line. These were awe-inspiring, memorable sights, images that will be with me all of my life. I dream of the low-country.

Many years, decades later, Pearce would return to the spawning-ground of the Georgia coast, and he would begin to court it with slavish attention and dedication, becoming the Thoreau of Savannah. Now an artist, he would sit and study the birds on shore and in tree limbs, and draw the sea-creatures, and ponder the workings of nature. He understood that when many parts make up a whole, each of them is important, often vitally so. He understood beauty. In the salt marshes Pearce knew contentment. He comprehended the affection that Thoreau described in his journals: "Here I am at home. In the bare and bleached crust of the earth I recognize my friend…"

I heard about Mallory Pearce before I met him. I have many friends on Tybee and some of them told me about a City Council member who ran for office on an environmental ticket and who was making waves. My friends were jubilant. This man voted for open space, he voted for wild trails, he voted for shorebirds, he voted for nesting turtles. (Pearce would serve a decade in this capacity.)

Then one day, in a moment that would begin a friendship, I ran into Mallory Pearce in a copy shop on Tybee. He was photocopying bird drawings and, indeed, reminded me somewhat of a tropical bird, with his mass of unruly curls and his intense eyes. As rain fell outside, we talked.

That encounter became a poem that, at its core, asked the question: In my life, has my allegiance rested with nature?

That is the question I keep asking myself.

This lovely and comprehensive book of natural history is Pearce's answer to that question. This book is a gift to the place that Pearce came to love and never stopped loving. Here is his loyalty, his patriotism, and his solidarity. Here is his allegiance.

> When I was in town, in the copy shop,
> I met the bird artist, local politician,
>
> whose errant gray curls plume from his head.
> For a few minutes, waiting to complete
>
> our business, we talked of birds. The drawings
> he showed me were simple and quick.
>
> What can I say I have
> accomplished in this life?
>
> Have I stayed true to the great blue heron
> balanced on one wand of leg,
>
> evenings, in the gray cedar,
> or to the wood storks
>
> with their hindrance of bills at ebb tide?
> Can I say I never abandoned them
>
> but was violent in my fidelity?
> This: when I left, the bird-man gracefully bent,
>
> kissed my hand, then waved me out
> into the rain.

MARITIME FOREST ON LITTLE TYBEE ISLAND

ACKNOWLEDGEMENTS

I am grateful to the following scientists who assisted me. Above all, I thank Eugene P. Odum (1913-2002), who encouraged me to do this book and gave me the overall ecosystem perspective. Christopher Schuberth (1933-2008) taught me about the geology of the coast during the many beach walks we took together. Francis Thorne, Professor of Botany at Armstrong Atlantic State University, reviewed the forest chapters and assisted me with specimens for the botanical illustrations. Janisse Ray reviewed the chapter on Longleaf Pine Forests.

The following wildlife biologists with the Georgia Department of Natural Resources critically examined the chapters on birds and mammals: James Ozier, Todd Sneider, and Brad Winn. Russ Webb, biologist at the Savannah National Wildlife Refuge, assisted me in preparing the chapter on freshwater wetlands. Cathy Sakas, biologist with Gray's Reef National Marine Sanctuary, reviewed and corrected the chapter on the beach and the sea. John Crawford, naturalist-herpetologist with the University of Georgia Marine Education Center and Aquarium, assisted me in many ways, especially in preparing material on reptiles and amphibians. I would like to thank Dave Chafin for allowing me to draw his live reptiles. And I would like to thank my wife Julia for her support.

Permission to reprint illustrations from my books was graciously given by Dover Publications.

MALLORY PEARCE
Tybee Island, Georgia

PREFACE

This book is a field guide to acquaint the amateur or professional naturalist with the coastal ecosystems, and the plant and animal life that live on the Southeast Coast of the United States. While that coast is in many ways similar to coastal habitats throughout the world, aspects of this ecology are unique and worthy of further study and enjoyment. The book covers the general features of coastal ecology and the most commonly observed plants and animals. It does not attempt to treat all of the plants and animals that can be found along the Southeast Coast. For those interested in more detail, the bibliography at the end lists several useful guides and references.

This book is organized into chapters covering each habitat, such as salt marshes, freshwater wetlands, and forests, but these habitats blend into each other and are dependent upon each other to maintain their well-being.

INTRODUCTION

During the Cretaceous Era, 90,000,000 years ago, the sea lapped along the edge of the Piedmont, what is known as the Fall Line. Since that time, the sea has receded. Ten thousand years ago, when Ice Age glaciers reached what we now know as Ohio, the shoreline was 100 miles east of its present location.

The expanse of sandy soil known as the Coastal Plain was once the ocean floor. Sand is really pulverized rock worn down and carried from the mountains to the sea by the rivers. Over centuries, the shoreline has advanced and retreated as the glaciers built up and melted. Erosion and build-up of the beaches still occur today, as you can see when strolling on the beach. While the Coastal Plains are enriched and fed by the flow from the mountains through the foothills to the sea, this book is limited to those habitats found in the Coastal Plains, the rivers that flow through the plains to the sea, and the coastal marshes and islands.

A unique geographic feature along the Southeast Coast is the indentation of the coastline, forming a large bay known as the "South Atlantic Bight," running from North Carolina to Florida. The stretch of coast from Hilton Head, South Carolina, to Jacksonville, Florida, is the most western section of the east coast of the United States, being ninety miles west of a line drawn from the coast of North Carolina to the southern tip of Florida. The bight forms a funnel, which concentrates the tide as it rises. The tidal extremes between high and low on the North Carolina Coast are about four feet. In the Florida Keys, the difference is one to two feet. On the Georgia Coast, the tidal difference is six to nine feet between high and low tides.

The interaction between the tides and the rivers flowing to the sea has produced a vast area, about 800,000 acres, of coastal salt marshes along the Georgia-Carolina Coast. The coastal salt marshes range from New England to northern Florida, but most of these marshes are a narrow strip, whereas the marshes on the Georgia Coast are twenty miles wide.

The climate along the coast is ameliorated by the adjacent ocean, so that it is neither as cold nor as hot as inland. The microclimate along the coast from South Carolina to north Florida has an average temperature a few degrees warmer than inland: subtropical with many palms and evergreen shrubs and trees. Southern Florida is tropical with many plants that will not tolerate frost. The coastal salt marshes are replaced by mangrove swamps.

The coast of North Carolina is transitional, as the beginning

viii

of the temperate, more northerly climate. Along the South Carolina-Georgia Coast, the continental shelf is wide, extending one hundred miles offshore. The continental shelf is only ten to twenty miles off Cape Lookout, North Carolina. The coastal islands are narrow and the sea is rougher.

I was introduced to the coastal Georgia marshes in 1950 when I moved to Tybee Island with my parents, as I was beginning high school. Tybee Island is on the coast at the mouth of the Savannah River. I grew up in upstate New York, a land of temperate forests, lakes, agricultural fields, and snowy winters, but I had always dreamed of going to the tropics, to the jungles and savannahs with their spectacular wildlife. When I turned fifteen, my dream came true. 1 was now living in a subtropical habitat with palms, evergreen oaks, magnolias, and expanses of marsh with spectacular birds: egrets, herons, and storks. Initially, my fascination was in the birds, but soon I became interested in learning as much as I could about the entire ecosystem.

Many scientists, ecologists, wildlife biologists, and naturalists helped me prepare this book. One scientist who had a major influence on my life and work was Eugene P. Odum, founder of the Institute of Ecology at the University of Georgia.

When I graduated from high school, I went to the University of Georgia and worked in Odum's laboratory. I originally wanted to be an ornithologist, and Odum had the reputation of being the best ornithologist in Georgia. However, he taught me a new word-ecology. When I entered his lab, Odum had just published the first edition of his seminal *Principles of Ecology*. While this book was not the first book on the subject, prior texts were either "plant ecology" or "animal ecology." Odum's book was the first to combine botany and zoology into a holistic approach emphasizing the "ecosystem." His ecosystem approach permanently influenced how I studied the natural world.

I completed my Bachelor of Science in ecology at the University of Chicago in 1957. At that time, few people knew what the word meant. However, I was in conflict between my interests in biology and art, so I changed fields and got a Masters of Fine Arts in Motion Pictures with a specialty in Animation at the University of California, Los Angeles. My thesis film was one of the earliest films explaining DNA with animation.

I worked in Los Angeles for thirty-five years making animated educational films on biology, medicine, and molecular biology, synthesizing my interests in biology and art.

I took the time to explore and study the western ecosys-

ix

tems: the Pacific Coast beaches and tide pools, the chaparral hills, the deserts, the mountains, the Redwoods, the Sequoia forests, and the Olympian rain forests. All of these are beautiful and interesting ecosystems, but my first love was always the coastal salt marshes of Georgia.

In 1990, I returned home to Tybee and continued my studies of the southeast coastal ecosystems.

Henry David Thoreau, whom I read in high school, has been a lifelong influence. As a result of reading Thoreau, I kept nature journals to record my observations, descriptions, and illustrations of the animals and plants that I discovered along the way. This book is the result of many years spent observing, studying, and keeping journals.

CONTENTS

I
MARITIME REGION

THE BEACH AND THE SEA
THE SCIENCE OF SAND

The beach, sometimes known as berm, is but a thin piece of sand between the vast and mighty ocean and the more inland solid land, the "terra firma." Yet the land adjacent to the ocean is not notably "firma" but is subject to changes from the forces of tides, winds, and storms. The beach itself is covered and then exposed by tides twice daily. Because of the funneling effect of the South Atlantic Bight, the southeastern coast of the United States has especially extreme tides, ranging from six to nine feet difference between the low and high tide mark with an average of seven and a half feet difference. If a storm occurs, especially a hurricane, the tidal surge can be higher. Twice a month, we have "spring tides" in which the tides are higher (nine feet as opposed to six feet). "Spring" in this case means "to spring or leap." Spring tide occurs during the full moon and new moon when the sun and moon are lined up and the gravitational pull on the earth and ocean is stronger.

The tidal flow also results in periodic erosion or accretion of the beach. In general, the fall and winter storms, especially the northeasterly winds, cause the beach to erode, but during the milder summer weather, the beach accretes, that is, it builds up.

Beach sand is really pulverized rock, primarily silicates (SiO_2) such as quartz. Over the millenia, quartz in the hills and mountains was worn away and floated down the rivers to the sea and was deposited as minute grains on the beaches. Most beaches also have deposits of "black sand," titanium dioxide (*rutile and ilmenite*). Black sand is heavier than quartz sand. As a result, wave action leaves bands of black sand spread across the beige-white quartz sand. This black sand is processed to produce the white titanium pigment used in paint or dyes to whiten paper or many other materials. Many of the illustrations of beaches have been prepared by using a product of beaches.

LIFE IN THE WAVES

Life began millions of years ago in the sea. and to this day, the sea is full of living things of which the majority are microscopic. Most of the sea's living things are hidden from our view beneath the surface of the water. However, the sea often deposits living animals or their skeletons on the beach where you can find them while beachcombing. Dolphins often break the surface of the water and sea turtles crawl onto the beach to lay their eggs in the sand. Many organisms. especially worms, crustaceans, and mollusks, live in the

2

wet sand of the intertidal zone. Seabirds and shorebirds probe the
wet sand seeking these animals as food.

The most abundant life forms in the sea are microscopic.
They form a dilute "soup" of organisms known as plankton. For
many larger organisms, even as large as bateen whales, plankton
becomes a soup that they consume for food.

Plankton consists of phytoplankton ("plants") and zooplankton ("animals"). Phytoplankton are primarily a variety of algae
species. Algae are photosynthetic; they synthesize sugars from water
and carbon dioxide using energy from the sun. The phytoplankton
are known as producers. The zooplankton are primarily protozoa
(single-celled animals) and microscopic multi-celled organisms, such
as copepods. Zooplankton eat the algae or often each other. They are
known as comsumers. Part of the plankton is microscopic larvae of
crabs, barnacles, and mollusks.

The zooplankton can propel themselves, while the masses of
plankton are carried along by ocean currents. Some larger organisms
are also carried by ocean currents and deposited on beaches, notably
jellyfish or sea jellies. Sea jellies do have pulsing wavelike movement,
but they are mostly carried along by current. Sea jellies are radially
symmetrical with a central mouth at the bottom of their bell-like
body shape. Their primary prey are small fish and other sea animals.
They capture prey with dangling tentacles covered with stinging
cells known as nematocysts. The nematocysts that are released by
the jellyfish are the cause of the stinging sensation felt by swimmers
who encounter jellyfish. Vinegar is a good antidote to the nematocyst
toxin.

Sea jellies primarily live in the open sea ("pelagic"), but periodically, in the summer, they wash up on the beaches where they
die. The most common sea jelly on the southeastern beaches is the
cannonball seajelly. Moon sea jelly and sea nettle will also wash up
on the beach. The stings on the cannonball are so weak that people
do not feel them, but the other two have strong stings. Be cautious;
leave the sea jellies where they lie.

Sometimes comb jellies wash up with the sea jellies. Like the
sea jelly, comb jellies have a gelatinous body, but they are smaller
than sea jellies; their bodies are spheroid instead of bell-shaped, and
they do not have stinging cells. Comb jellies glow in the dark when
stimulated ("bioluminescent"). However, sea jellies and comb jellies
are not related. Jellyfish are in the phylum *Cnidaria* (which means
having "stings") or *Coelenterates* whereas the comb jelly is in a different phylum known as *Ctenophora*.

The Portuguese man-o-war is primarily a tropical species,

3

but a few are carried by the Gulf Stream up to the Georgia-Carolina waters. This sea jelly is a colonial animal consisting of hundreds of organisms attached to a single colony. Its tentacles may be sixty feet or longer. This is the most dangerous jellyfish, and the stinging is very painful. The favorite diet of sea turtles is jellyfish, including man-o-wars. Sea turtles are immune to the nematocyst toxin.

Echinoderms periodically wash up on the beach. The phylum *Echinodermata* (meaning spiny-skinned) includes sea stars, sand dollars, sea urchins, and sea cucumbers. These are radially symmetrical animals with a central mouth containing grinding teeth. Most of them eat algae, small invertebrates, and carrion. However, sea stars, sometimes known as starfish, are ravenous carnivores that prey on bivalves, including clams and oysters. The sea star wraps its arms around the bivalve. On the underside of its arms are rows of small tube feet that have suction cups at their ends. The sea star can glide along with the help of these tube feet, but the suction cups of the feet also help by prying open the bivalves. The sea star then inverts its stomach into the open bivalve and digests it. In the past, fishing people who harvested clams or oysters tried to get rid of the sea star that preyed on their harvest by cutting them into pieces and discarding them in the water. But each piece of starfish would grow into a complete animal. Inadvertently, the fishing people were increasing the starfish population.

The flat sand dollar, otherwise known as the keyhole urchin, buries itself in the sandy bottom. Sea cucumbers are shaped like a cucumber with a mouth at one end. If disturbed, sea cucumbers excrete their entrails. However, they survive this action and new entrails re-grow.

Sponges often wash up on the beaches. The animals are firmly attached at the base (sessile). However, currents may knock them loose, so they wash up on the beach. Sponges are the simplest of the multi-celled animals. Basically, a sponge consists of several layers of cells upon a skeleton, which is often tubular in form. This skeleton may be made of silicate, calcite, or a flexible protein known as spongin, as in a bath sponge. The cells inside the skeleton have threadlike mobile projections ("cilia") from the cell surface. The cilia move in waves that propel the seawater through the pores and hollows of the sponge, and the cells absorb plankton or microscopic debris, also known as detritus. The word "detritus" is from Latin meaning to "rub away" or decay. Tube sponges, redbeard sponges, and finger sponges are found on the southeastern beaches. When still alive, some of these sponges have brilliant colors, but they quickly fade. The boring sponge wraps itself around bivalves, such as oysters

4

and clams, and "eats" holes in the shells. Boring sponges are rarely found on the beach, but evidence of the activity of these sponges is common: shells full of holes.

The beachcomber is looking for shells on the beach, basically skeleton remains of animals in the phylum *Mollusca*. The two most common Molluscas on the beach are snails and bivalves.

Snails have one large, flat, muscular foot that lets them glide along the sand. The stomach is just above this muscular foot. Thus, the technical name for snails is *Gastropod*, which means "stomach foot." Several eyes are mounted on tentacles. Although some snails exist without shells, known as slugs, the typical snail has a spiral-shaped shell. The snail can withdraw its whole body into this shell and close the door with a hard oval covering known as an opercu-lum. Many snails are vegetarians or carrion-eaters, but many other are carnivores. Snails have a "tongue" known as a radula that is cov-ered with hard spines. Several species of snails use the radula to drill into other shells, then secrete digestive enzymes and suck out the contents of its prey. Moon snails, auger snails, and oyster drills ob-tain their food by this method. Often, a beachcomber can find many shells on the beach with clean round holes in them. These holes are the result of drilling by snail radulae.

Snails vary in size and shape from the small algae-eating periwinkle to the large carnivorous whelks. Whelks come in three local types: channeled whelk, knobbed whelk, and lightning whelk. The lightning whelk has a left-handed twist to their shells, while the other two have right-handed twists.

The illustrated pages that follow portray many snail shells that can be found on the Georgia-Carolina beaches. Two snails that do not resemble the usual snail are slipper shell and baby's ear. The slipper shell feeds on plankton filtered from seawater. It usually remains stuck on hard objects, such as oysters, horseshoe crabs, or other slipper shells. Baby's ear is a spiral, but it is flat. The ear shell is enclosed within the slimy body of the snail. The baby's ear snail bur-ies itself in the sand.

Some snails have specialized egg cases. Whelks have a series of sacs strung together. The moon snail produces a "sand collar" full of eggs.

BIVALVES & BARNACLES

Bivalves are abundant on the beaches. Most often, the beachcomb-er finds single shells, but the living bivalve has two shells at-tached by muscles that can close the shell tightly. Bivalves, otherwise

5

known as *Pelecypoda*, are filter-feeders. They filter plankton from seawater. Most are buried in mud or sand in the ocean floor.

The scallop, however, is mobile. By repeatedly snapping its shells shut, it produces a jet stream so that the scallop bounces along the ocean bottom.

The smallest bivalve is the cocina and it buries itself in the sand, often at the edge of the surf on the beach. Most bivalves, including clams, cockles, scallops, and ark shells, bury themselves singly, but some bivalves, notably oysters, are colonial. They attach to each other, forming a colony. The shell-less oyster larvae are microscopic, part of the plankton. The oyster larvae attach to a solid surface: a dock post, rock groins, jetties, mud banks, or other oysters. When they grow, they develop their shells. When the tide is out the oysters are tightly closed. When the tide is in, they open and obtain their nourishment from the plankton. Mussels often associate with oysters, attaching to the oyster shells; mussels also form clusters in the marsh mud. Oysters and mussels are both favorite food items among human populations, but many other bivalves are quite edible.

Barnacles attach themselves to oyster colonies. Although they look like mollusks, barnacles are related to crabs. The microscopic barnacle larvae, part of the plankton, closely resemble crab larvae. When they reach a hard surface, say, a rock, a post, an oyster, a sea turtle carapace, or a whale back, they attach and develop their shell. Like bivalves, barnacles are filter feeders. Their legs have become cirri which move to generate water currents that carry the plankton upon which they feed. Like bivalves, barnacles close during low tide and open to feed during high tide. Two basic kinds of barnacles are known: acorn barnacles, the most common type, and goose-neck barnacles that have a long flexible stalk.

CRABS/CRUSTACEANS

Except for the ghost crab. which lives in the dunes, most crabs live under water on the bottom, but they can be found in the tide pools that form around jetties or groins. The hermit crab, which resembles a lobster, is quite common in tide pools.

The hermit crab has a soft body and chooses to live within snail shells for protection. As it grows, it will seek a larger snail shell and abandon the old shell as it switches its rear into the new shell. Most crabs stay in the water, but their carcasses or carapaces often wash up on the beach. The illustrations at the end of this chapter show several species of crab that a visitor might find on the beach.

Crabs, shrimp, lobsters, and crayfish are classified as a sub-

6

group of crustaceans known as decapods (ten legs). Amphipods and isopods are small crustaceans that differ from decapods. The common garden animal known as a sow bug, pill bug, or roly-poly bug is an isopod.

The animals that crawl through and over beach debris that are known as sea roaches and beach fleas are not insects but isopods. Tiny isopods and amphipods live in the wet sand at the edge of the sun. The shorebirds that probe in the sand are seeking these diminutive animals as food.

Larger crustaceans that live in the sand at the water's edge are the mole crab, one-half to one inch long, and the ghost shrimp. Both feed on plankton and detritus. At the water's edge, we may find a series of tiny holes surrounded by brown particles. These holes were made by ghost shrimp. The particles, like bits of chocolate, are the shrimp's feces. The mole crab lives in the wave-washed area of the beach. They dig into the wet sand, leaving their snouts exposed to receive the food brought in by the incoming waves.

The last crab in this section is not really a crab. The horseshoe crab is related to spiders. *Chelicerata* denotes that it has claws. The horseshoe crab is an ancient animal that has lived in the ocean for 600 million years, a "living fossil." It dwells on ocean bottoms, ranging from shallow water to seventy-five feet in depth. Spines on its legs grind the food so it eats as it walks. It preys on mollusks, worms, and small crustaceans. It has six pairs of book gills that function in air or water.

From spring to early summer, horseshoe crabs come out of the water to mate. Males follow the females onto the beach, where the females dig a hollow, lay their eggs, and the males deposit sperm on the eggs. Then the eggs are covered with sand by the female. The females mate multiple times during the season, producing as many as 20,000 eggs. Horseshoe crab eggs are favorite food items with shorebirds. When horseshoe crabs hatch in late summer, they are the size of quarters. As they grow, they shed their shells multiple times before reaching full size. The periodic shedding of shells is known as molting. We can often find the molted shells of horseshoe crabs or true crabs on the beach. They are sexually mature in nine to ten years.

WORMS, CORAL & SEA LETTUCE

Sharing the sand with cocina clams, mole crabs, and isopods are several species of polychaete worms, which are segmented worms (*Annelida*) related to earthworms. Some polychaetes are swimmers; others are bottom crawlers. While many polychaetes are buried naked in the sand, several encase themselves in a covering. These coverings, minus the living worm, may end up on the beach. At times, beachcombers can find masses of what looks like spaghetti or linguini. These are the discarded cases of soda straw worms, so called because of the appearance of the casing. The plumed worm leaves a casing encrusted with tiny shells. Sometimes, the visitor may find bivalve shells that are encrusted with sinuous calcareous tubes, which were made by hard tube or mason worms. The tubes are the worm's home, not the worms themselves.

The tide pools that form around groins or jetties contain sessile forms of *Cnidaria*: anemones and hydroids that attach to a hard surface. *Cnidaria* have two basic body shapes. The medusa form is like the sea jelly, bell-shaped with dangling tentacles. The polyp form is attached to a surface (sessile). Its body is cylindrical or tubular. At the top of this cylinder is a circular row of tentacles surrounding a central mouth. Polyps capture prey with these tentacles. Most hydroids are small, less than an inch, but the tubelarian hydroid, which resembles a flower, may be six inches long. The anemones are larger than hydroids; their bodies are thick cylinders rather than slender tubes. Anemones can contract their tentacles like a fist when disturbed or if the tide leaves them exposed. Anemones are attached (sessile) but they can move by gliding along their base.

Coral are underwater animals whose skeletons can wash up on the beach. They are colonial polyps. Their skeletons have indentations where the polyps resided. The star coral is hard and calcareous, often encrusted on bivalve shells. Each polyp had left a star-like indentation, up to thirty per colony.

Sea whips are slender and branched like a tree branch with small pits where the polyps resided. Sea whips are colorful: red, yellow, purple, or tan.

The strangest-looking coral is the sea pansy. It resembles a thick water lily pad with a tail. The pad is covered with circular pockmarks where the polyps resided.

On groins and in tide pools, can be found sea lettuce, an algae that resembles its namesake, and a leafy brown plant-like organism known as a *Bryozoan*. This "plant," however, is not a plant, but an animal. *"Bryozoan"* means *moss animal.* Most of what we see is a plant-like skeleton; the living part is a tiny animal (zooid) about one half millimeter long. It resembles a polyp with a circular ring of tentacles around an open mouth. *Bryozoa* eat plankton. Like corals, bryozoans are colonial with numerous zooids living on the branching skeleton. Bryozoan larvae are microscopic and are part of the plankton.

TUNICATES

The strangest invertebrates are a group known as the tunicates. Tunicates are not really invertebrates but are members of the phylum *Chordata*, which includes the vertebrates. During some stage in their life cycle, all chordates have a notochord, a hard rod that runs down the back, and a nerve cord (dorsal) parallel to the rotochord. In the vertebrate embryo, the notochord is replaced by the vertebral column (the backbone) that encloses the dorsal nerve. The name "Tunicate" comes from the external covering known as a tunic. Tunicates are filter feeders.

A strange-looking creature that may wash up on the beach is the sea pork, so-called because it resembles a piece of meat. It is flat, sometimes lumpy, usually pink, one inch thick, and as much as one foot wide. It is a colonial animal made up of many small zooids. It is a tunicate, a chordate. When we gaze at this strange-looking flat "piece of meat," it is hard to imagine that this animal is our closest relative among all the invertebrate animals found on the beach. It is normally a deep-water animal, but it occasionally washes up on the beach.

Sea squirts and sea grapes, globular in shape, are sessile tunicates that attach to pilings and docks under water, often on floating docks. They are called sea squirts because they squirt water when their sides are squeezed.

VERTEBRATES

What vertebrates might one see on the beach? Fish are the most abundant vertebrates in the sea, but it is rare to see them from the beach. Sometimes you might see minnows, silversides, or killifish in the tide pools. Skates or stingrays are sometimes stranded on the beach. These are primitive fish; generally, triangular in shape with wide pectoral fins and long thin tails. The stingray is an inoffensive and non-aggressive fish. The stinging tail is only used defensively. If stepped on, they lash out with the tail.

Sharks and rays are cartilaginous fish, that is, their skeletons are made of cartilage rather than bone. Most of the inshore sharks are small and harmless. The ominous white shark is a rare visitor to the coasts of Georgia and Carolina. However, on some beaches, the beachcomber can find fossil shark's teeth, especially on beaches where dredging happens in nearby channels or rivers. The fossil teeth, many thousands of years old or older, are black. An illustrated plate that follows shows you the various fossil teeth.

Sharks and rays are ancient fish, 400 millions years old — older than the dinosaurs. Modern bony fish are about 360 million years old. Although people rarely see a bony fish from the beach, such fish can be caught by rod and reel, casting net or seine net. The most commonly caught inshore fish are flounder, sheepshead, sea trout, whiting and mullet.

This chapter does not attempt to cover the vast field of marine biology. For those interested, there are many books on the subject. Peterson's Field Guide, *Atlantic Coast Fishes*, by Robbins et al is a good reference.

MAMMALS

The inshore fish attract many fishing birds and bottle-nosed dolphins. Since the dolphin is a mammal, it must frequently come to the surface to breathe. Sometimes the dolphin leaps out of the water. The dolphin is a very intelligent social mammal that depends on an elaborate system of vocalizations to communicate with one another. Although dolphins have excellent eyesight, they also use echolocation, similar to radar, to find their way in murky waters and to seek prey.

A group of dolphin, known as a "pod," can consist of up to twelve dolphins or more, but occasionally dolphins gather in super-pods of up to one thousand individuals. Often males and females associate in separate bands.

Like all mammals, the young of dolphin are born live. They will suckle from their mothers for up to three to five years. Gestation period is twelve months, and most births occur in spring or fall. Sexual maturity in females occurs between five and fifteen years of age; males reach sexual maturity eight to thirteen years. Dolphins are estimated to live up to forty or fifty years.

Dolphins are toothed whales that eat fish and squid. They often herd fish and stun them by whacking them with their flukes. They can find buried fish by echolocation and dig them up with the rostrums, the nose. Their nostrils are at the top of their heads, the "blow hole." The most interesting method of feeding is when the dolphins chase a school of fish onto a mudbank, then beach themselves to gobble up the fish. Dolphins do follow fish up the narrow tidal creeks of the marsh. Dolphins are opportunistic feeders and will gather around to capture the "bycatch" (non-shrimp fish) that shrimpers throw overboard as they sort out the daily catch. In places where people feed them, dolphins will approach boats and stick their heads out of the water to beg. Most biologists and ecologists discourage dolphin-feeding, and it is a federal offense in the United States to feed dolphins.

The largest whales are baleen whales. Baleen are long rows of plates made of fingernail- like material that hang from the roof of the mouth. These plates capture masses of plankton and small organisms, such as krill. The baleen whales remove this mass with their tongues and swallow it. The right whale is a baleen whale that migrates along our coast. They mate in the spring off the New England coast. In late fall, they migrate south along the coast to a locale just off the Georgia-Florida border. While there, the females give birth to their calves in the winter.

This whale is called the "right" whale because it was the "right" whale to hunt. Since it is a slow swimmer, the whaling ships could easily catch them. They are now protected, but they are only slowly recovering from years of being hunted. At present, about 400 individuals exist.

The current threat to the right whale is collision with ships. The slow-moving whale cannot get out of the way of the faster ships

The other sea mammal that we may see off the Carolina-Georgia Coast is the Florida manatee. They prefer warm waters, but during the warm summer months, a few migrate north. Manatees are vegetarians. European sailors that came in the 1500s and 1600s thought that manatees were mermaids.

SEA TURTLES

The other vertebrates that regularly come ashore from the sea are sea turtles. Five species of sea turtle come to the Georgia-Carolina Coast: loggerhead, green, hawksbill, kemp, ridley, and the giant leatherback. The loggerhead is the most abundant.

During the summer months, the female loggerhead crawls up the beach to the seaward side of the sand dunes. She digs a pit and lays about 100 to 150 leathery eggs, then buries them and returns to the sea. The young turtles hatch in forty-five to eighty days, dig themselves out, and go to the sea, usually at night. Light is their cue; they waddle to the sea, which is brighter than the land. Artificial light may distract them. When they cross the beach, they run the gamut of predators: ghost crabs and raccoons. If they go during the day, they are prey to seabirds. Once in the sea, baby loggerheads are subject to other predators. In thirteen to thirty years, the fully-grown female sea turtles that survive return to the beach where they were hatched to lay their eggs in turn.

11

The sea is vast and the number of its organisms is vast. This chapter is designed to help beachcombers identify what they may find on or near the sea. The following chapters describe the dunes and the birds that may be seen on the beach or over the sea.

Beaches & the Sea

CNIDARIA
formerly known as Coelenterates

CORALS

Star Coral living animals
Astrangia davae

Tubelarian
Hydroid

Sea Pansy
Renilla
reniforms

Sea Whip
Leptogorgia
virgulata

detail

red, yellow, purple
or tan

Anemone

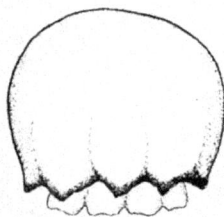

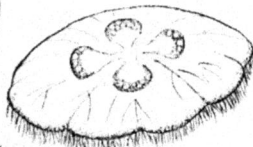

Sea Nettle
Chrysaora
quinquecirrha

Cannonball Sea
Jelly Stomolophus
meleagris

Moon Sea Jelly
Aurelia aurita

Echinoderms

Forbes Sea Star
Asterias forbesi

tube feet

Slender Sea Star
Leptasterias tenera

Sea Cucumbers will
extrude theirs "guts"
if disturbed

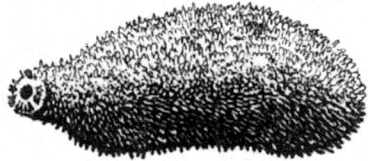

Sea Cucumber
Sclerodactyla spp.

Urchin test
"skeleton"

Keyhole Urchin
or Sand dollar
*Mellita
quinquiesperformata*

Sea
Urchin
Arbacia punctulata

Porifera

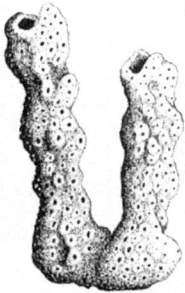  

Tube sponge
Aplysina fistcelaris

Red Beard Sponge
Microciona prolifera

Finger Sponge
Haliclona oculata

   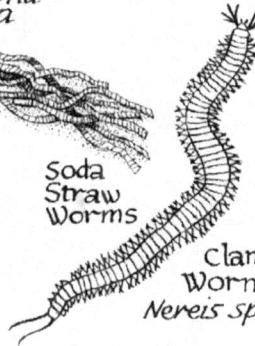

barnacle
lacy bryozoan
Mason Worms

Plume Worm

Soda Straw Worms

Clam Worm
Nereis spp.

Polychaetes

Sea Grape
Molgula manhattensis

Pleated Sea Squirt
Styela plicata

Sea Pork
Amaraucium stellatum

Tunicates

Snails

Olive Snail
Oliva sayana

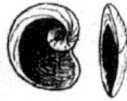

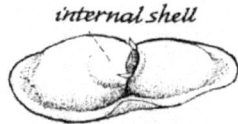

internal shell

Living Baby's Ear

Baby's Ear *Sinum perspectivum*

Moon Snail *or* Sharkseye
Polinices duplicatus

Slipper Shell
Crepidula spp

Sand collar:
moon snail
egg case

Tulip
Fasciolaria spp.

Oyster drill	Auger	Chestnut Turban	Periwinkle	Nutmeg
Urosalpinx cinerea	*Tenebra discolata*	*Turbo castanea*	*Littorina irrorata*	*Cancellaria reticulata*

WHELKS

Knobbed Whelk
Busycon carica

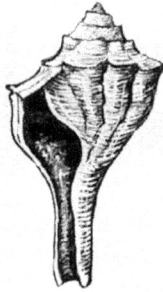

Lightning Whelk
Busycon contrarium

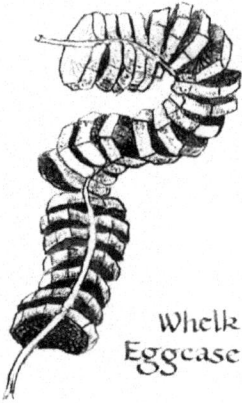

Whelk
Eggcase

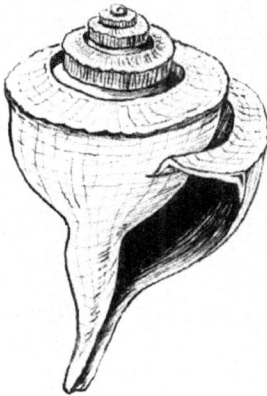

Living Whelk

Channeled Whelk
Busycon caniculatum

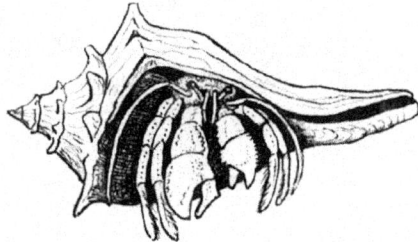

Hermit Crab in Whelk shell
Pagurus spp.

BIVALVES

Great Heart Cockle
Dinocardium robustum

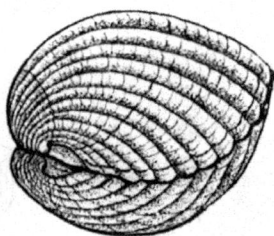

Living cockle

Arc Shell
Noetia ponderosa

The arc shell is straight with teeth
The cockle is curved

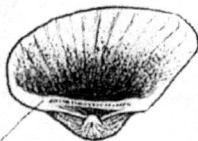

Sawtooth
Penshell

Atrina sp.

Young clam

Quahog Clam
very thick shell

Ribbed Mussel
Geukensia demissa

Stiff Penshell
Similar to above
but with tubular
projections.

BIVALVES

Jingle Shells
Thin, translucent shells
Black, gray, white or ochre
Anomia simplex

Surf Clam
Spisula solidissima

Prickly Cockle
Trachycardium sp.

Cocina
These are the smallest bivalves
Donax variabilis

Dwarf Surf Clam
Mulinia lateralis

Cross-hatched Lucine
Divaricella quadrisulcata

Cat's Paw
Plicata gibbosa

Jewelbox
Aricinella cornuta

King Venus Clam
Chione paphia

Bittersweet Clam
Glycemeris americana

Piddocks are small bivalves that bore into wood.
Barnea truncata

BIVALVES

Jackknife
Clam
Tagelus spp.

Razor Clam
Ensis directus

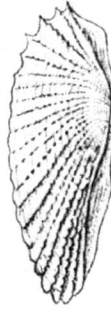

Angelwing
*Cyrtopleura
costata*

False
Angelwing
*Petricola
pholadiformis*

Disc Clam
Dosinia discus

Tellin
Tellina alternata

Channeled Duck Clam
Raeta plicatella

Scallop
Argopecten irradians

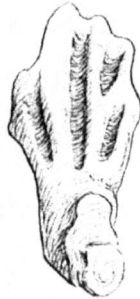

Oysters
Crassostrea virginica

CRABS

Blue Crab
Callinectes sapidus

Stone Crab
Menippe mercenaria

Speckled Crab
Aranaeus cribrarius

Dolly Varden or Calico Crab

Hepatus epheliticus

Purse Crab
Persephona mediterranea

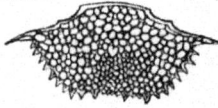

Lady Crab
Ovalipes ocellatus

Spider Crab
Libinia spp.

Horseshoe Crab
not a true crab but
related to spiders

Limulus polyphemus

21

Acorn Barnacles

Balanus spp.

Goose Barnacles

Lepas spp.

Mole
Crab

Emerita spp.

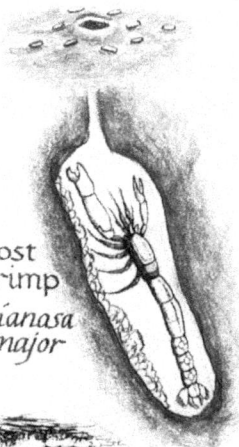

Ghost
Shrimp
*Callianasa
major*

Isopods

mating Horseshoe Crabs

22

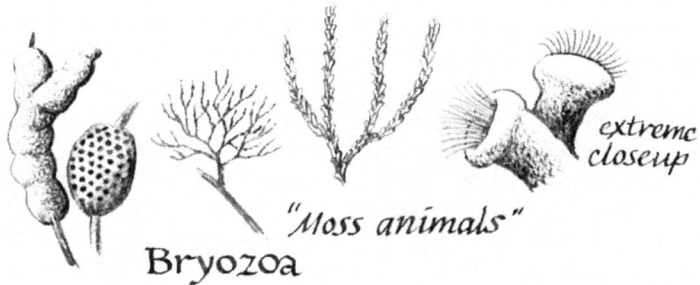

extreme
closeup

"Moss animals"
Bryozoa

Comb
Jelly
Mnemiopsis
leidyi

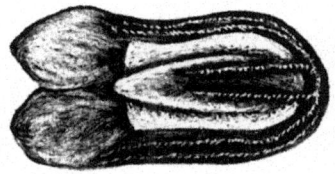

FOSSIL SHARK'S TEETH

Carcharhinus
specie

Tiger
Shark
Galeocerdo
cuvier

Giant
White
Shark
extinct
Carcharodon
megalodon

Sand shark
Odontopsis
taurus

Mako
Shark
Isurus spp.

Clearnose
Skate
Raja eglanteria

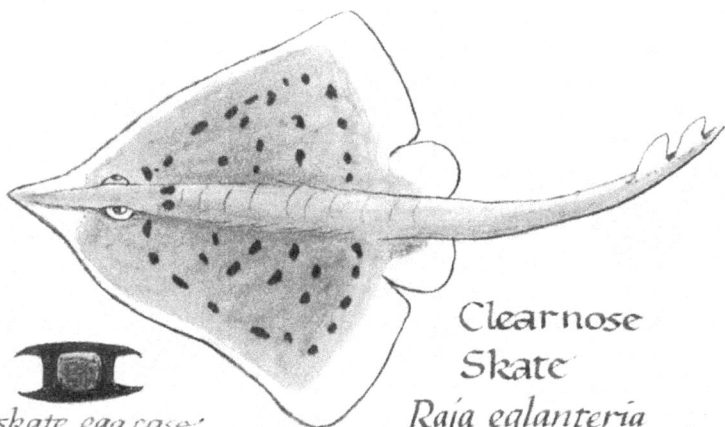

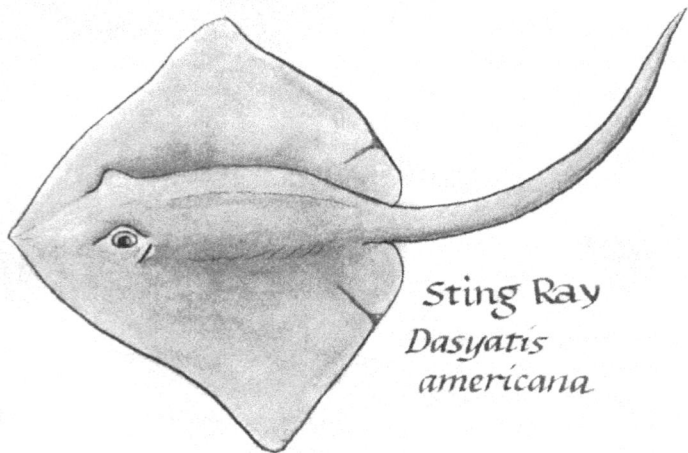

skate egg case

Sting Ray
*Dasyatis
americana*

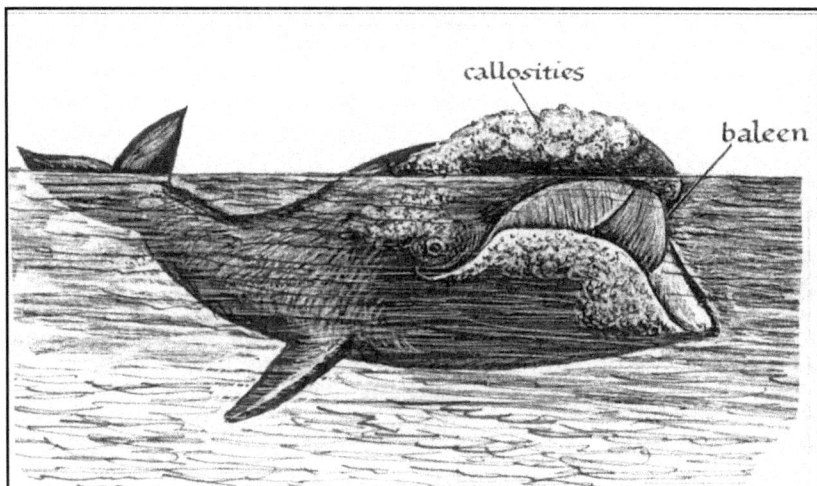

callosities

baleen

Right Whale
Eubalaena glacialis

Nurse Shark
Ginglymostoma cirratum

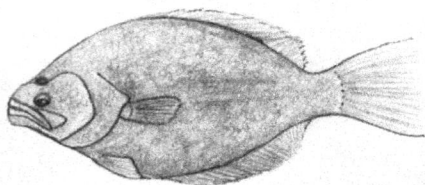

Flounder
Paralichthys spp.

Sheepshead
Archosargus probatocephalus

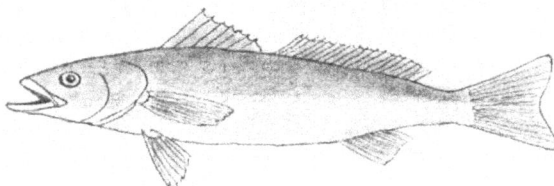

Seatrout or Weakfish
Cynoscion spp

Kingfish or Whiting
Menticirrhus americanus

Mullet
Mugil cephalus

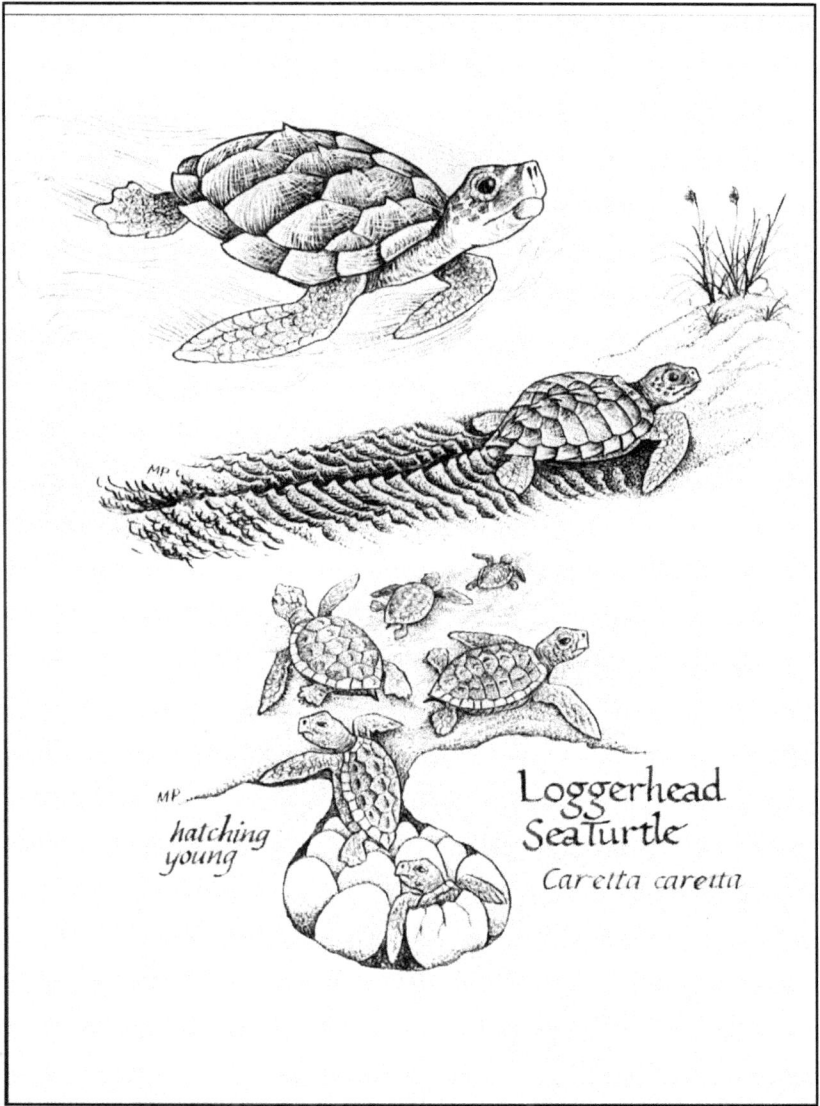

hatching
young

Loggerhead
SeaTurtle

Caretta caretta

Bottlenose Dolphin
Tursiops truncatus

Florida Manatee
Trichechus manatus

THE DUNES AND INTERDUNE MEADOWS

The dunes are among the most unstable of the coastal ecosystems. They are constantly being created, moved, or destroyed by the action of wind and waves. On some coastal islands, the dunes are gone. The sea has conquered the forest, leaving a "graveyard forest" of whitened, skeletal trunks of twisted oaks, cedars, or tall, straight pines, sometimes mounted on a pedestal of exposed roots. However, on the same islands, we can find areas with rows of dunes and wide beaches in front.

Thanks to wind and tides, dunes and beaches are always in motion, accreting, or eroding. If left alone. dunes will always be there. but they may have moved. During the summer. the dunes and beaches usually are built up, but during the storms of late summer through winter, erosion occurs. In many cases, the sand is moving back and forth between the beach and offshore sandbars. Another factor contributing to beach accretion is the flow of sand carried by the tide north to south. Harbor deepening, however, interrupts this flow and may cause beach erosion.

The main problem that affects the coming and going of the dunes is the construction of permanent beachside dwellings and hotels. With our penchant for controlling nature, humankind has built seawalls, revetments, groins, and jetties. These artificial devices work for a while, but ultimately they succumb to the relentless force of the tides.

In the meantime, the beach may be destroyed when waves hit a seawall. The energy is repulsed back to the sea, carrying the sand with it so that the beach disappears.

The best remedy to protect the beaches and nearby houses is a healthy dune system, not just one row of dunes but a system with several rows of large dunes. When a storm surge hits a dune system, the energy will be dissipated. When the waves recede, they carry sand back, thus naturally renourishing the beach.

DUNE PLANTS

Dunes are created by wind action. The straw-like wrack (dead stalks of marsh cord grass washed up on the beach) collects the wind-blown sand and the seeds of the dune plants, which stabilize the dune. Dune plants have a unique adaptation: they are among the few species of plants that can be totally covered with sand and continue to grow.

The reason people are kept out of the dunes is to protect the dunes and their plants. Crowds of walkers could destroy the dune plants and subject the dunes to wind erosion. Although the coast has more rain than the desert ecosystem, dunes are desert-like because sand does not hold water. The dune plants have desert-like adaptations. Many dune plants store water by having thick, succulent leaves as, for example, the evergreen seaside elder (*Iva imbricata*). Another adaptation is a deep root system reaching to underground water, such as that of sea oats (*Uniola paniculata*). Sea oats are the dominant species of dune grasses.

Another common dune grass is panic grass (*Panicum amarum*). Two virtually identical species of very short grass grow in the dunes: dropseed grass (*Sporobolus virginiana*) and spike grass (*Distichlis spicata*). Beachgoers are often annoyed by the spiny seed capsules of the sandspur (*Centrus* spp.).

Sprawling over the dunes in long runners is the fiddleleaf morning glory, bearing white flowers with a yellow center. The grasses and the morning glory die back in winter, then produce new green leaves in spring.

One of the significant ecological concepts is plant succession: new land is colonized by pioneer species, followed by a succession of plant species until the climax habitat is reached. In the maritime forest, pines are replaced by the climax species, the live oak. Since dunes are always being created, plant succession is always happening. Sea oats and seaside elder are dune climax species.

Pioneer plants often grow seaward of the first row of primary dunes. An interesting pioneer plant is the succulent sea rocket (*Cakile edenfula*). It is an edible plant with a cabbage-like flavor (both are in the mustard family). In the spring, the sea rocket springs forth from the sand as single plants or small clusters. By summer, they are gone.

Another edible dune plant is the sea purslane (*Sesuviun portulacastrum*). This plant spreads out and forms extensive dense mats.

The Russian thistle, another pioneer plant, remains all through the summer but becomes dry and covered with thorny seed capsules. It was accidentally introduced from Russia, along with its close relative, the tumbleweed.

DUNE ANIMALS

The dominant resident animal in the dunes is the ghost crab, which lives in deep burrows dug in the sand between the dune mounds. Although it sometimes comes out in the day, it is most active at night. Primarily a scavenger, the ghost crab will eat live prey, such as young sea turtles. The ghost crab lives on land, but it needs to keep its gills wet. At night, it runs into the ocean. It also digs its burrow below the water line. It is quite fast and usually can reach its burrow before anyone catches it. Its scientific name, *Ocypode quadrata*, means fleet-footed. The ghost crab spawns in the ocean, and the microscopic larvae become part of the plankton.

Terns, gulls, and some shorebirds will nest among the dunes, and many birds will feed there. Redwing blackbirds, grackles, and sparrows eat the seeds of the sea oat, and painted buntings will eat the seed of panic grass. When dunes are extensive, interdune meadows may occur, which are distinctive ecosystems of their own.

The salt meadow cord grass (*Spartina patens*, a thin-leaved grass) is a dominant plant. In the fall, the coastal meadows can be full of flowers: *Gallardia* (red and yellow) is common. The naturalized Lantana with its orange and yellow flowers flourishes in the dune meadows. These flowers attract the orange butterflies that migrate through in the fall. Although the region has some monarchs, most are Gulf fritillary butterflies and longtailed skippers (brown and blue). In some cases, the dune meadows develop dense thickets of shrubs, especially wax myrtle or southern bayberry (*Myrica cerifera*). The wax-myrtle thickets are important habitats for small birds, such as wintering warblers and painted buntings. The prickly pear cactus (*Opuntia* spp.) grows in the dune meadows or at the edge of the adjacent maritime forests. Yucca, another desert plant, grows in the same habitat.

On some coastal islands, oak forests are growing on the leeward side of the dunes.

In addition to being key ecosystems, extensive large dunes and dune meadows are the best protection against storm surges.

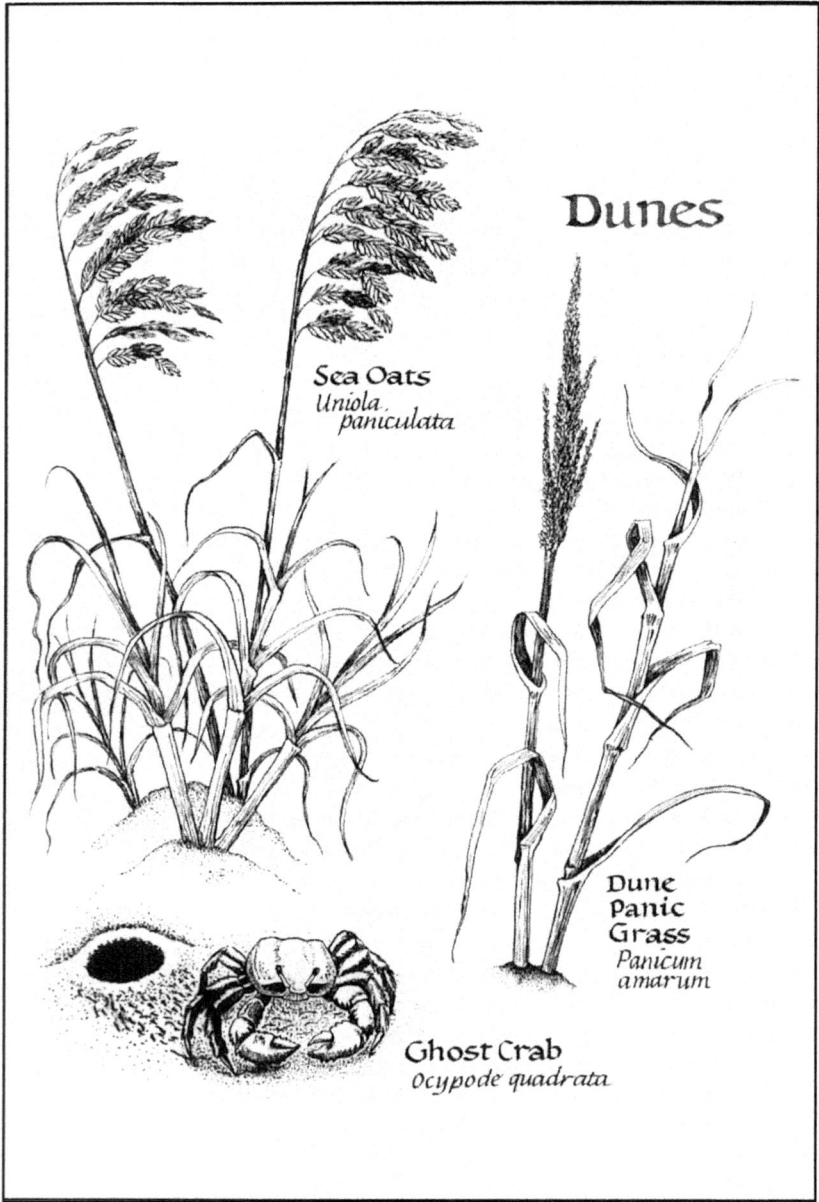

Dunes

Sea Oats
Uniola paniculata

Dune
Panic
Grass
Panicum amarum

Ghost Crab
Ocypode quadrata

Sea Oats on dunes

Seaside Elder
Iva imbricata

Fiddle-leaf Morning Glory
Ipomoea stolonifera

Dune Plants

33

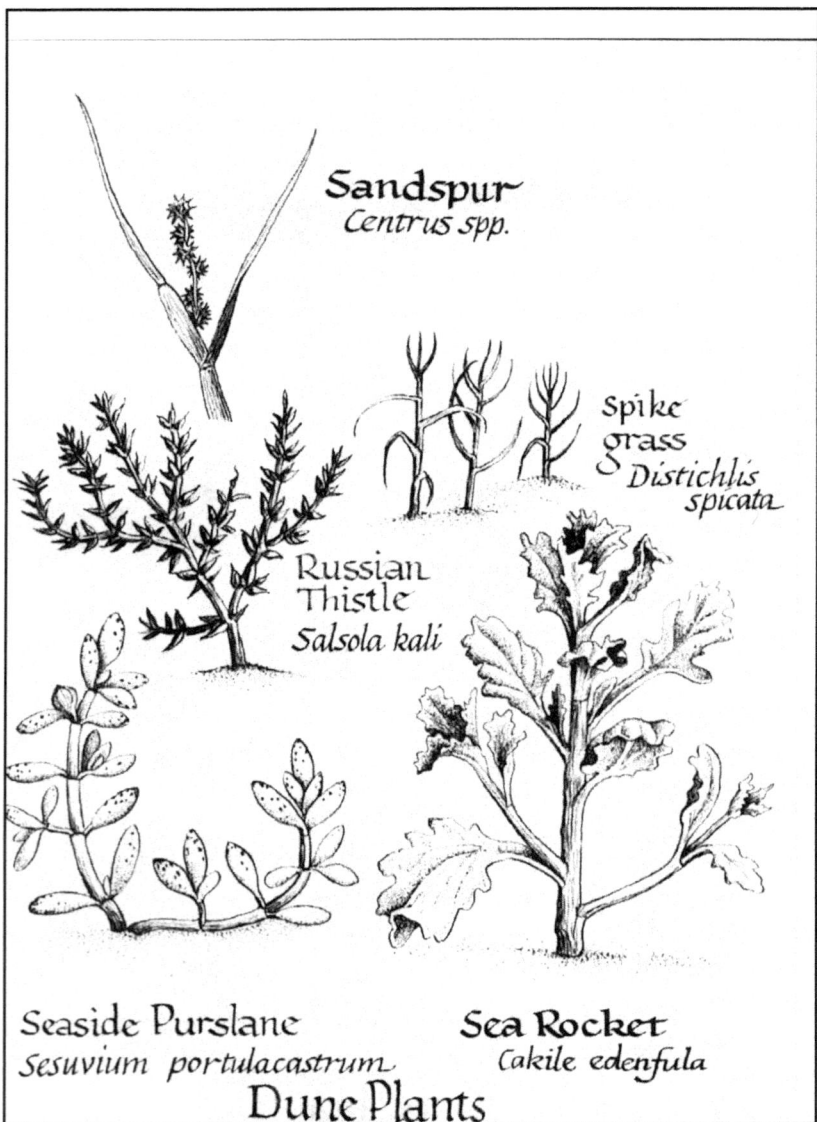

Sandspur
Centrus spp.

spike
grass
*Distichlis
spicata*

Russian
Thistle
Salsola kali

Seaside Purslane
Sesuvium portulacastrum

Sea Rocket
Cakile edenfula

Dune Plants

34

Gulf Fritillary

Monarch

Longtailed Skipper

Prickly Pear
Opuntia spp.

Lantana

Gaillardia
pulchella

Wild Flowers

Most of the flowers grow in open areas: roadsides, dune meadows or edges of forests or marshes.

Rattlebush

Daubentonia punicea

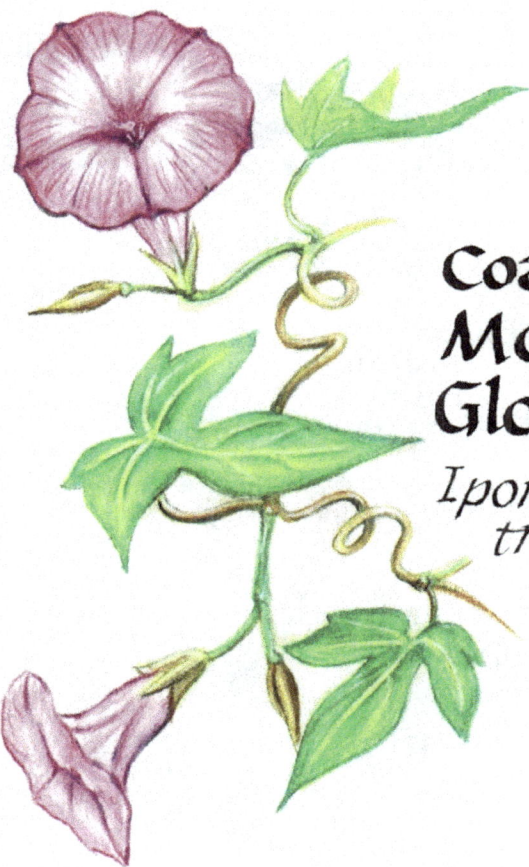

Coastal
Morning
Glory

*Ipomoea
tricarpa*

Vetch
Vicia spp.
a vine

Evening
Primrose
Oenothera spp.

Trumpet vine
Campsis radicans

Gerardia *or*
False Foxglove
Agalinus fasciculata

Butterfly pea
Clitoria mariana
a vine

Cardinal-spear
or **Coral Bean**
Erythrina
herbacea

may reach 7 feet in
heigth - flowers and leaves
grow on separate stalkes.
often grows in shade.

Painted Leaf
or **Wild Poinsettia**
Euphorbia cyathophora

Camphorweed
*Heterotheca
subaxillaris*

seedhead

Skullcap
*Scutellaria
integrifolia*

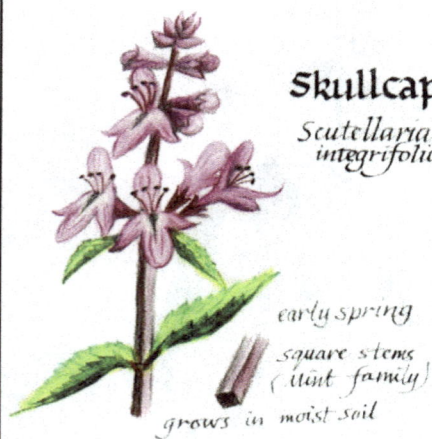

early spring

*square stems
(mint family)*

grows in moist soil

Goldenrod
Solidago spp.

Toadflax
Linaria canadensis

early spring

Spiderwort
Tradescantia virginiana

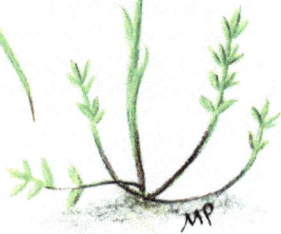

41

Pennywort or Dollarweed *Hydrocotyle*

white flowers

Bull-Nettle
Cnidoscolus stimulosus
Don't touch!
This plant stings

Wood Sorrel *Oxalis*
Yellow: *O. stricta* Violet: *O. violacea*

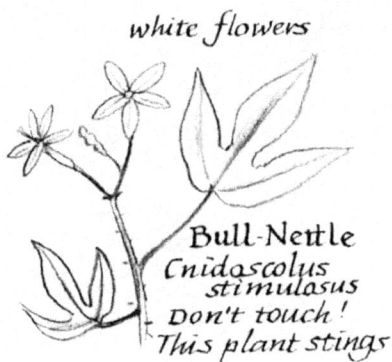

SHOREBIRDS

During the winter months, thousands of shorebirds, sandpipers, and plovers gather on the Atlantic beaches, running at the edge of the surf, often stopping to probe in the sand for food. Their food is small invertebrates like isopods, amphipods, insects, minute mollusks, and worms.

Although a few shorebirds nest on this coast, the majority nest in the tundra of the far north. The summer season in the tundra is short, so they will spend the season on the southeast coast from late summer through the winter to late spring.

The most commonly seen sandpiper on the coast is the sanderling. This bird is eight inches long, russet in summer, pale gray and white in the winter. They usually run together at the edge of the water, but sometimes they act aggressively with each other. Aggressive behavior is probably related to a scarcity of food resources. They look like mechanical toys; their rapidly moving feet are a blur, as their bodies seem to glide smoothly above their moving feet. Then the sanderling stops abruptly and probes in the sand.

The sanderling nests in the furthest northern tundra in Alaska, Canada, Greenland, and Siberia. In the winter, it can be found on virtually every beach in the world, except Antarctica.

Often associated with sanderlings are dunlins. Gray in winter, the dunlin's bill is longer than the sanderling's and slightly down-curved at the tip. In the spring and summer, the dunlin wears resplendent plumage: a russet back with a black patch on its belly. Worldwide in distribution, the dunlin's range is similar to the sanderlings.

Another common wintering shorebird on the Atlantic coast is the ruddy turnstone. Nine and one-half inches long, it has a calico plumage pattern with orange legs. In the spring and summer, its back is russet. Its feeding pattern is different than the sandpipers. It often turns over stones or other debris looking for food; hence its name. It digs holes and will eat birds' eggs. Turnstones like to gather in small groups to forage on rock jetties. The range of this bird is similar to the sanderling.

These three species are common sandpipers on the Atlantic Coast during the winter, but other species show up during fall and spring migration. In fact, the overall numbers of shorebirds are larger during migration.

The red knot is variable in its population on the coast, but it is most numerous during the fall and spring migrations. It is a large shorebird, ten inches in length, pale gray in winter, russet red in summer. During the spring migration, the flocks bear both russet and gray plumages plus many in intermediate molting plumages.

Another large wintering sandpiper, eleven inches, is the dowitcher, distinguished by a very long bill. However, these birds prefer to forage in tight flocks on mud bars where they probe deeply in the mud with their long bills. They nest in Canada and Alaska. Two species of dowitcher exist, the short-billed and long-billed, though both species have long bills. The short-billed dowitcher is the species most commonly seen in salt-water habitats.

Three wintering species of very small sandpipers, six to six and one-half inches, are known collectively as "peeps" or "stints." The western sandpiper is the most numerous of these species. The bill of this sandpiper is turned down at its end. The semi-palmated and least (yellow legs) sandpipers are less common on the Southeast Coast. The peeps are sporadic when they show up. However, I have observed flocks of up to one thousand western sandpipers on the beach on Tybee Island, Georgia.

The whimbrel, also known as a curlew, is a large sandpiper, seventeen and one-half inches, with a long down-curved bill. Flocks of whimbrels gather on isolated locales on the southeast coast during winter or migration.

The purple sandpiper, another tundra nester, winters in small groups of six to twelve, usually hanging out on wave-washed rocks. It winters farther north than other shorebirds: from Canada south through the Carolinas to the mouth of the Savannah River at Tybee Island. It is uncommon south of the Savannah River. The winter plumage is overall gray, not purple; it has a dull orange spot at the base of the bill and dull orange legs.

The spotted sandpiper nests in freshwater marshes, ponds, and lakes throughout most of the United States and Canada, but in the Southeast, it is primarily a winter visitor, staying close to the coast. It is rarely found on the beach, preferring the coastal salt marshes. It is a solitary bird, "teetering," raising and lowering its tail like a seesaw, while feeding on mudflats, or flying low over the water with a flap-glide flight.

The willet, fifteen inches long, is the only sandpiper that breeds on the Georgia-Carolina-Florida Coast. It is a common resident and will nest on coastal islands in the marsh above high tide, even on inland lakes. The nest typically contains four to five eggs and is built from grasses, rushes, and sedges. It is a plain gray bird, but when it raises its wings, it reveals a striking black and white pattern.

The other group of shorebirds is known as plovers. The killdeer commonly found throughout the United States in open fields,

44

is a plover. Several small species of beach plovers, seven inches, are known as ringed plovers because of a black ring around the neck. The semi-palmated plover is the coast's most common wintering plover, often found with sanderlings. The piping plover is an endangered species. It nests on eastern beaches from Canada to North Carolina. Many miles of piping plover nesting sites have been lost to beachside development. If not for scattered coastal wildlife refuges, we would lose the piping plover altogether. The semi-palmated plover nests in the tundra, which is not under threat of development.

Another ringed plover, the Wilson's plover, nests on uninhabited islands on the Georgia-Carolina Coast. Their nests are scrapes in the ground above high tide, sometimes lined. The usual clutch is three eggs, and they sometimes nest colonially.

A plover found on the coast in the winter in moderate numbers is the black-bellied or gray plover, eleven and a half inches. In the winter, it is gray, but in the spring and summer, it is black underneath, from the face to the belly, with a speckled back.

One of the most interesting coastal birds is the oystercatcher. It is seventeen and a half inches long, black and white with a long red bill. They feed on oysters, other bivalves, crabs and other invertebrates. Their bill is built like a reinforced wedge with a triangular cross-section. If the oyster or clam is partially open, the birds insert their bill and rapidly, within thirty seconds, sever the bivalve adductor muscles. The other method is hammering, shattering the shell with a series of rapid blows. They hammer open crabs as well.

Oystercatchers often hang out in pairs, on beaches, mudflats, or oyster reefs, but they may roost together in large groups.

The nest, usually with three eggs, is no more than a shallow scrape in sand or gravel. The nesting pair creates a solitary nest on a beach or marsh edge, occasionally nesting colonially.

Flocks of running and feeding shorebirds are a delight to any beach visitor. Feeding birds can tolerate human visitors on a beach. However, shorebirds need isolated, protected areas, free of human, or canine, disturbances, to nest and reproduce. If we still want to enjoy shorebirds on our beaches, we need to make sure their breeding locales are protected.

SEABIRDS

GULLS

Gulls, commonly called "seagulls," are certainly the most numerous seabirds in the world. Some species of gulls are equally at home on inland lakes.

Gulls are bold and aggressive. They have omnivorous eating habits: fish. invertebrates, fruit, and carrion. They are opportunistic and will readily steal food from other birds or glean such leftover food as French fries, pretzels, crackers, and bread. They become bold with human beings, gathering to pilfer leftover food or swarming around a person tossing food, sometimes catching the food in mid-air, accompanied by raucous screams. Gulls will swoop down to the water surface to catch a fish, or fly into a palm tree to pluck berries off a palm frond, but, whenever possible, they prefer found food, scavenging dead fish on the beach, stealing human food, or food from other birds, especially terns who are excellent fish catchers.

Gulls will stomp on wet sand, loosening the sand to release buried worms or other invertebrates. They eat other bird eggs and nestlings. Gulls are social birds, but they frequently engage in aggressive displays with each other, either to establish dominance ("peck order") or to protect a food source.

The most common gull is the ring-billed gull, a gray and white gull with a black ring around its yellow bill (length: seventeen and a half inches). On a long stretch of beach on Tybee Island—about one and a half miles—I have counted 2000 or so ring-billed gulls. The ring-billed gull is resident year-round, but it only breeds in Canada and a few northern states. Most of this coast's resident ring-bills are immature. It takes about two to three years for gulls to reach maturity. First-year gulls are dark gray. They go through several molts before reaching adult plumage.

Scattered among the ring-bills on some beaches are a handful of large herring gulls, twenty-five inches. Like the ring-bills, the immature herring gulls are dark gray, reaching the adult gray and white plumage in three years. Less numerous in the Southeast, the herring gull on the northeast United States Coast is abundant to the point of being a pest, often destroying other bird colonies. Gradually, this gull is extending its range south, now nesting as far south as North Carolina.

In the winter, the Southeast has a few lesser and greater black-backed gulls. The greater is the region's largest gull, thirty inches. The black-backed gulls are also extending their breeding range south to North Carolina.

Although herring and black-backed gulls nest in North Carolina, the laughing gull is the most common nesting gull in the Southeast. Its nesting range extends from New England to Florida. Its nesting areas vary from beaches to high marsh above the high tide. It is a small gull, sixteen and a half inches, with a black head and a dark gray back. In the winter, the black hood is reduced to a dark spot behind the eye. The name "laughing" comes from its sound: a high-pitched maniacal pulsing "laugh." Like most seabirds, the laughing gull nests in colonies, producing an average of three eggs at a time. The nest is simply a scrape in the sand, lined with grass and sticks. Initially, the young are fed by regurgitation of the parents.

The one other gull that is a regular on the Georgia Coast is the Bonaparte's gull. This gull is small, thirteen and a half inches, with a black head in summer. However, this gull only visits Georgia and the Carolinas in the winter. The black hood then is reduced to a black spot behind the eye. The distinguishing feature is a white wedge on the leading edge of the wing. The bird was named for Charles Bonaparte, an ornithologist who wrote scientific treatises on the classification of American birds. He was also Napoleon's younger brother.

TERNS

In contrast to the opportunistic, scavenging gulls, the terns, relatives of the gulls, only catch live fish. Sometimes known as "dive-bombers," terns hover, and then dive, catching a fish in their sharp pointed beaks. Five species of terns are resident on the Southeast Coast. Unlike the gulls, no tern will approach a human being to beg for food.

The terns nest communally in mixed species groups, including black skimmers, pelicans, and laughing gulls. They like to nest on isolated islands, usually sandbars, isolated from human beings and egg snatchers, such as raccoons.

Royal terns are the most abundant terns on the Southeast Coast: about 40,000 breeding pairs. This tern is twenty inches long, gray and white with a black cap and crest and an orange bill. They usually lay one egg in a scrape in the sand. During courtship, the male struts before the female with neck extended and chest elevated. As part of the courtship ritual, the male gives a fish to the female, which she displays for awhile before swallowing. Only after that will the female allow the male to mount her.

The sandwich tern nests communally with the royal tern. The sandwich tern is slightly smaller than the royal tern, fifteen inches. It has a black bill with a yellow tip. About 20,000 breeding pairs of sandwich terns are on the Southeast Coast. The gull-billed tern is a rare breeder in the Southeast. There are only 650 pairs on the Southeast Coast (250 pairs in North Carolina, 300 pairs in South Carolina, 50 pairs in Georgia, and 50 pairs in Florida). Its bill is black, short, and thick, hence the name, "gull-billed". Terns' nests are but scrapes in the sand, sometimes bare, sometimes lined. The clutch is typically one to two eggs.

The largest of the local terns is the Caspian tern. It resembles the royal tern, but its large beak is bright red. Although the Caspian tern does nest on a few sites on the Atlantic Coast, it is a fall-winter visitor on most of the coast. It associates in flocks with the royal and sandwich terns, but the numbers are smaller than the other two species. The Caspian tern is a worldwide species; its name is taken from the Caspian Sea between Russia and Iran.

The least tern is our smallest species, 9 inches, and is a summer resident only. It nests on isolated beaches, with an average of two eggs. In many parts of the United States, it is an endangered species because its beach nesting sites have been developed for human use. However, the least tern often nests on the flat gravelly roofs of markets and other stores, especially if these roofs are near water. About 25,000 least terns exist in the Southeast.

The least tem associates only with itself, avoiding the larger gulls and terns. However, in August, the migrating and small black terns will roost in groups with the least tern. These birds breed in freshwater marshes in the north and pass through here before moving south. They stay a few weeks; then they are gone to reappear the next August.

The Forster's tern exists in the Southeast in moderate numbers, 1000 to 2000. It nests as far south as North Carolina, but from South Carolina through Florida, it is primarily a winter visitor. In the winter, a black patch behind the eyes replaces its black crown.

SKIMMERS

The most unusual seabird on the Atlantic coast is the black skimmer. This bird is black and white with red feet and beak. Its beak is unique among birds: the lower beak is longer than the upper beak. Skimmers are also found in Africa and Asia. These three species are the only birds with this unusual beak. Their feeding habits are unique: they fly low over the water, usually in a linear flock, trailing their long lower beak through the water surface. When the lower beak encounters a minnow or small crustacean, it automatically snaps shut. They really skim for their supper. This interesting adaptation led Mark Catesby and other eighteenth-century ornithologists to call them "cutwaters." A skimmer may break rank from its flock, circle around, and pick up food from the surface of the water. Usually, skimmers are nocturnal feeders, but during the nesting season,

48

they also feed during the day.

About 25,000 nesting pairs are on the Southeast Coast. They may nest colonially with terns. The young are fed by regurgitation at first, but as they mature, they are brought small whole fish. Each nest, a scrape in the sand, has three to four young. Initially, the young have short beaks, the top and bottom the same length. Gradually, as they grow, the bill lengthens. They do not develop the long lower beak until they are ready to fly. As they grow, the young leave the nest and run about.

Although only a few spots exist on this coast where they nest, resting flocks of gulls, terns and skimmers can be found anywhere on the coast. All the birds in these flocks face the same way: into the wind. If they need to fly, they simply raise their wings, and the wind lifts them into the air.

PELICANS, GANNETS & CORMORANTS

Often found in the same breeding colonies with the terns and skimmers are brown pelicans. They congregate only on isolated islands, but they wander up and down the coast as far north as Virginia. Two to four eggs are laid in the nest, which is but a scrape in the sand. In the 1960s and 1970s, the population of pelicans declined precipitously, due to thinning of eggshells caused by DDT. In 1972, DDT was banned, and the population of brown pelicans has recovered.

The other species of pelican in the United States is the larger white pelican, primarily found in lakes and freshwater marshes of the West and Midwest. The white pelican winters in south Florida and the Gulf Coast. It is a regular winter visitor to the Georgia-Carolina Coast. I have seen winter flocks of fifty white pelicans resting on a mud bar not far from Cumberland Island, Georgia.

Most of the world's seven species of pelicans, including the American white pelican, fish from the surface while swimming. The brown pelican, found on both coasts of North and South America and the Caribbean, is the only species of pelican that dives for fish. They hit the water with open mouth. When they come to the surface, they squeeze out the water and swallow the fish. Adult pelicans feed the young predigested regurgitant.

The Northern gannet is a pelican cousin that visits the Southeast Coast in the winter. They nest on rocky cliffs in the Northeast and Canada. The gannet also dives for fish, but it is a power dive. The bird follows the fish underwater and swallows it. The pelican just drops into the water and scoops up the fish with its fishnet bill.

49

We can observe both pelicans and gannets fishing together during the winter. Pelicans frequently follow one another in a line, but the gannet soars individually in wide circles. Large groups of gannets, fifty to one hundred, regularly gather to fish offshore, but they never form tight flocks like the pelicans. During the winter, gannets never come ashore; they are either soaring or swimming.

Both pelicans and gannets are excellent soaring birds, though their wings are shaped differently. Soaring birds need to have wings designed to reduce drag. Gannets have a wing shaped like an albatross, long and narrow, coming to a point. The pelican wings have many points as represented by the spread primary feathers, known as "slotting." Vultures, eagles, and hawks also have "slotted" wings. Both wing designs successfully reduce drag. Pelicans and gannets are excellent gliders, soaring over the ocean with only an occasional flap.

Double-crested cormorants, distant relatives of pelicans and gannets, are abundant in winter and summer from New England to Florida and the Gulf Coast. The Canadian population of these birds flies south for the winter. They catch fish by chasing them underwater, and they often perch on posts or trees spreading their wings to dry. Their wing feathers absorb water, which helps the birds stay underwater, so when they come out, they need to dry their feathers. They are widespread in the ocean, salt and freshwater marshes, rivers, and lakes.

Sometimes swimming with the cormorants, superficially resembling them, are loons. Loons nest in freshwater lakes in Canada and the northern United States, but about seventy percent of loons winter in the coastal waters of the Atlantic, south of Cape May, New Jersey and the Gulf Coast: 500,000 common loons and 70,000 red-throated loons.

(Reference: *Southeast United States Regional Waterbird, Conservation Plan* by W.C. Hunter, W. Golder, S. Melvin, and J. Wheeler)

50

Seabirds & Shorebirds

Greater Black-backed Gull
The lesser black-backed gull is smaller with yellow legs.

winter

Bonaparte's Gull

Ringbilled Gull

adult

winter

Laughing Gull

immature

adult

immature

Herring Gull

Gulls

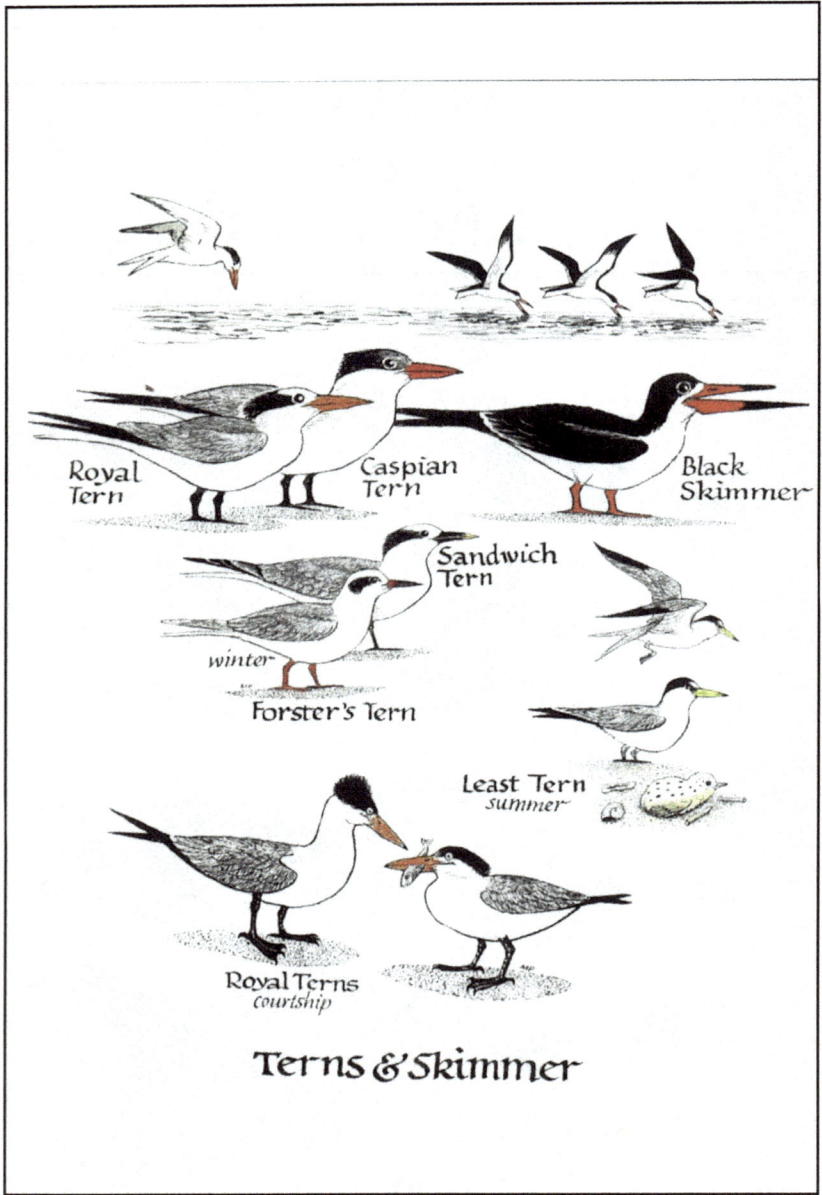

Royal
Tern

Caspian
Tern

Black
Skimmer

Sandwich
Tern

winter

Forster's Tern

Least Tern
summer

Royal Terns
courtship

Terns & Skimmer

Black Skimmer *with young*

half-grown skimmer

fledged juvenile

adult   immature

Gannet

Brown
Pelican

White
Pelican

Double
crested
Cormorant

adult

immature

Gannet

Common
Loon

Red-throated
Loon

summer loon   winter loon
cormorant

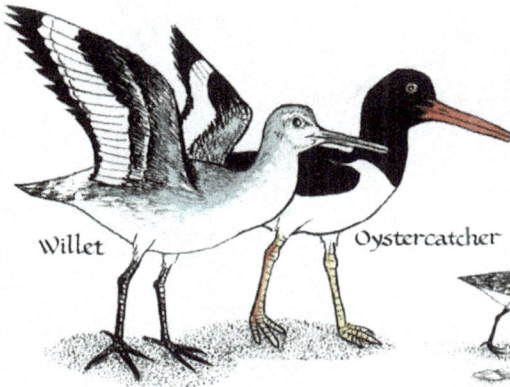

Willet

Oystercatcher

Shorebirds

Western **Sandpipers**

summer

Knots

Sanderlings

winter *summer*

Dunlins

winter *summer*

Ruddy Turnstones

Spotted Sandpiper

Whimbrel   Long-billed Dowitcher

Purple Sandpiper
found on or near the groins

winter   summer

Blackbellied
Plover

Semipalmated
Plover

Piping Plover
endangered

Wilson's Plover

II
WETLANDS

COASTAL SALT MARSH

SALT MARSH FOOD CHAIN

The salt marshes on the coasts of Georgia and South Carolina are among the unique landscapes of the world. Georgia has approximately 500,000 acres of coastal marsh; South Carolina has about 380,000 acres. The coastal salt marshes of North Carolina and northern Florida are but narrow bands.

Salt marsh is the most productive ecosystem on earth, producing 2500 grams of biomass per square meter per year, as opposed to 2,000 grams for tropical rain forest and freshwater wetlands, and a mere 700 grams for agricultural lands. A major industry depends on the salt marshes, namely, commercial and recreational fishing. In particular, marshes provide nursery grounds for white and brown shrimp, blue crab, red drum, spotted sea trout, spot, and croaker.

The bottom of the food chain in salt marshes is microscopic plankton and detritus. The primary source of detritus is decayed stalks of marsh cord grass (*Spartina alterniflora*). Only a few animals, such as insects and periwinkle snails eat cord grass directly. Only after it dies, decays, and turns into detritus, a process taking about a year, does cord grass become the major food source for marine life.

The next level of the food chain includes worms and other invertebrates that live in the bottom mud. The invertebrates are the primary food source for the rapidly growing juvenile fish, shrimp, and crabs that live in the tidal creeks. Marsh cord grass (*Spartina alterniflora*) is the dominant plant of the coastal salt marsh, especially in the lower, regularly flooded parts of the marsh.

Adjacent to the creeks, cord grass may grow six feet or more. In those areas far from the creek, where only high tides reach, cord grass is short, one foot or less. The height of cord grass is determined by the amount of nourishing water it receives daily. In the high ground mud flats, flooded only in very high tides, small succulent plants grow, primarily glasswort or pickle weed (*Salicornia*) and salt wort (*Batis martima*). These two succulents only grow in salt water. Both are edible, tasting like salty pickles.

Marsh cord grass will grow in fresh water. However, it is rarely found in fresh water because it cannot compete with the dominant freshwater plants, such as cattails. Cord grass has the capacity to excrete salt. If we examine the cord grass leafblades, we will find small white grains of salt. If we touch the leaf with the tongue, we will recognize the salty taste.

Other plants grow in the higher ground of the marsh: the evergreen, succulent (nonedible) sea oxeye (*Borrichia frutescens*),

58

which bears yellow daisy-like flowers in the summer, and the sharp-pointed black needlerush (*Juncus roemerianus*). At the marsh fringes, we have the thin-leaved salt meadow cord grass (*Spartina patens*) and a small tree or shrub, groundsel tree or cotton bush (*Baccharis halimifolia*). The cotton bush is distinguished by puffball seed heads in the fall. The seeds, each with its own gossamer parachute, are dispersed by the wind like dandelion seeds.

The marsh cord grass is the dominant plant, covering seventy-three percent of the salt marsh. Cord grass primarily spreads vegetatively, sending out runners like most grasses. It does flower every August to September. The stigma "female part" is white, which produces a white frosting on the fields of cord grass. If we examined a flowering stalk, we would notice the white stigmas alternate with the male stamens bearing particulate brown pollen, hence the scientific name, *alterniflora*.

MARSH LIFE, BIRDS

The salt marsh is home to many species of wildlife: two fish-eating mammals, the otter and mink. Although the raccoon invades the marsh to fmd food, its primarily home is on dry land. Many birds, such as egrets, heron, ibis, storks. and osprey, inhabit wetlands. both fresh and saltwater. and wooded swamps, as well as lake edges and rivers. One bird is restricted to cord grass salt marsh: the marsh hen, officially called the clapper rail. A close relative, the king rail, is restricted to freshwater marsh, the freshwater marsh hen. The California subspecies of the clapper rail is listed as an endangered species, because little of the cord grass salt marsh is left in California. The few places on the California coast where cord grass marsh remains have populations of California clapper rail. The mangrove clapper rail of south Florida is also endangered due to the destruction of mangrove swamps. Although the marsh hen will occasionally eat small fish, its primary diet is aquatic invertebrates, such as insects and snails. The bird is shy and elusive, usually escaping detection, but we can hear its resonant cackles. The marsh hen is a prolific breeder, producing five to twelve fuzzy black chicks, twice each season.

John James Audubon described its behavior in his book *The Birds of America* published in 1842: "On the least appearance of danger, they lower their head, stretch out the neck, and move off with incomparable speed ... they have a power of compressing their body to such a degree as frequently to force a passage between two stems so close that one could hardly believe it possible for them to squeeze themselves through."

Rails can escape by swimming underwater. Incidentally, Audubon called them "salt water marsh hens."

I once had an encounter with a mother marsh hen and her chicks. I was walking along an overwalk across the marsh when I startled a cluster of chicks that scattered in all directions. The distraught mother lept upon the overwalk and charged me with lowered head and spread wings. I backed up and left the courageous mother alone with her young.

The California and mangrove clapper rails are declining due to loss of habitat. However, the clapper rail of the Southeast Coast still has a thriving and healthy population. The marsh hen population will remain healthy as long we continue to preserve and protect the coastal salt water marsh lands.

Another distinctive bird of grassy marsh, both salt and fresh water, is the marsh wren. Though not a water bird, it spends its entire life in the marsh, living in grass above the water level. In the spring, its bubbling trilling song erupts from the marsh. The male sings atop a grass stalk, singing with its tail cocked at an angle. The male builds the nest, a spherical construction interwoven with marsh grass. As part of his courtship ritual, he builds several nests, hoping to attract a female. When the female shows up, she picks one and finishes the interior. Then they begin to raise their summer brood (four to six).

The redwing blackbird nests in the salt marshes, but it will nest in all grassy wetlands, even in dry grasslands. This bird is among the more abundant bird species in the United States. In the winter, it gathers in large, unisex flocks, but during the breeding season, the redwing establishes nesting territories. The female builds the nest of grasses or other fibrous material interwoven among the marsh grass or other marsh plants. The female takes care of the nesting duties, while the male stands guard on the highest perch he can find, singing, his red epaulets often erect. Typically, the pair is monogamous, but the male may stand guard over two and sometimes three females. They raise three to four young during the summer months. Their diet is grass seeds and insects.

Several species of sparrows reside in the marshes, most of which are winter residents. The seaside sparrow breeds in the salt marsh, ranging from New England to north Florida, as well as the Gulf Coast. However, its distribution through the salt marsh is patchy, and it is a secretive bird. It prefers areas where the marsh grass is not tall, as well as *Salicornia* mud flats, black rush (*Juncus roemerianus*) and groundsel tree (*Baccharis halimifolia*). Nesting season runs from April to August. The clutch is two to five eggs. The eggs hatch after twelve to thirteen days of incubation, and the young fledge nine to ten days later. Sometimes, the nests of different breeding pairs are placed close to each other. Neighboring pairs are usu-

60

ally very tolerant of each other and rarely exhibit outward aggression. The diet of the seaside sparrow includes seeds, insects, spiders, and fiddler crabs.

The savannah and sharp-tailed sparrows join the seaside sparrow in the southeastern coastal salt marshes only in winter. However, they hide out in the grass, and are hard to see. The song sparrow, another winter resident, likes to hang out in the marsh-side shrubbery. It is distinguished by a nasal "chip" call note.

A common marsh bird is the belted kingfisher. This bird is found wherever water is available with fish: marshes, lakes, swamps, and rivers. It will hover above the water until it spots a fish, and then dive into the water to retrieve it. It will perch on overhanging branches or telephone wires, peering into the water below. When the bird spots a fish, it dives from its perch. It is extremely territorial. A pair will defend a territory where they can fish. The pair will chase away any invading kingfishers, uttering their loud, rattling call.

The belted kingfishers build their nests in cavities dug into mud banks near water. Occasionally, they use tree cavities. They raise one brood per summer, usually six to seven young. As soon as the young learn to fish, the adults chase them from their territory. In the Southeast, kingfishers are permanent residents. This is one bird in which the female is more brightly colored than the male. The female has rust-colored swatches on her breast; the male's breast is pale and plain.

CRABS

Among the more abundant animals in the coastal marshland are the fiddler crabs. While no accurate count of the population of fiddler crabs on the southeast coast may be available, the estimate is one million per acre. In round figures, the Georgia-Carolina Coast has about 800,000 acres of coastal marsh, which means that about 800 billion fiddler crabs are on that coast! Their range is widespread from Massachusetts to the Gulf Coast. Fiddler crabs are worldwide in distribution. Seventy-nine species are classified in one genus (*Uca*). On the Georgia Coast are three species: the brackish water fiddler (*Uca minax*), the sand fiddler (*Uca pugilator*), and the mud fiddler (*Uca pugnax*).

The brackish water fiddler is found upriver where the salt water is mixed with fresh water. The brackish water species is the largest of the three. It has been reported to attack and eat the smaller species.

All of the fiddlers live on mud flats subject to tidal action, but subtle differences in their microhabitats occur. The brackish fiddler prefers less saline waters. The sand and mud fiddlers will live

61

together, but they have different tastes as far as the substrate they live upon. As the name indicates, the mud fiddlers prefer mud, while the sand fiddlers live on substrates varying from a sand-mud mixture to almost pure sand.

The mud fiddler usually has a brown carapace, but the carapace of the male sand fiddler is violet to pink.

The fiddler's home is the inter-tidal zone that is covered with water during high tide, and exposed during low tide. Fiddlers are most active during low tide; feeding, displaying, courting, and wandering about. They live and hide in burrows, often building a "chimney" about the burrow entrance. During cold weather, fiddlers remain in their burrows in hibernation, only coming out when the weather warms up (in the 80s F).

The fiddlers, like all crabs, breathe through gills. As long as the gills remain wet, the fiddler will do fine on dry land, or to put it more accurately, wet mud. The fiddlers remain in their burrows if the mud is dry and cracked, presumably to keep their gills from drying out.

The fiddler's diet consists of particulate matter, such as algae, microorganisms, detritus, and decayed plant material. The females have two small claws with which they alternately pick up food and thrust it into their mouths, looking like small children cramming food into their mouths with their hands. The fiddler's mouth with its attached appendages separates the edible organic material from the mud and sand, leaving behind tiny, round pellets.

The males, however, have one enlarged claw and one small claw. They feed themselves with the small claw. Their name "fiddler: comes form this claw, because it looks as if the crab is holding a fiddle. However, the "fiddler claw" is as long as the crab is wide. In relation to its body size, this claw is equivalent to a cello. This "fiddle claw" is useless for feeding; it is only used for displaying. The male fiddler spends most of its adult life waving at other crabs. Its enlarged claw can be on either side; fiddler crabs are either right-handed or left-handed. Rarely, a male fiddler is born with two enlarged claws. I have observed fiddlers struggling to eat with the smaller of the claws.

The center of the male fiddler's world is his home burrow. Although he will wander about looking for food or mates, most of the time he stands by the entrance, waving. The home burrows are a few inches to a foot or more apart. The male fiddler's hole and the mud surrounding it are his personal property. He makes every effort to keep other males away. Fiddlers sometimes interlock claws and engage in a shoving match, or they may move back and forth, towards and away from each other, as if establishing a property line. However, these aggressive activities only happen occasionally. Most of the time, the male fiddler stands by his hole and waves, like a public announcement: "This is my property! No trespassing!" This proprietary wave is deliberate. As the male elevates his claw, he stands on tiptoes. As he sinks back down, he returns his claw in a circular motion to its lower rest position. These waves are spaced one to two seconds apart.

The female's behavior is different. They wander freely over the mud bank, shoving food into their mouths, and seek shelter, when alarmed, in the nearest hole. As the female meanders over the mud, the males engage in a frenzy of activity, waving frantically at the passing female. If the male is lucky, the female will follow him into his home burrow or the male will hustle the female ahead of him into the burrow.

Copulation usually occurs within the burrow,which can be as deep as two feet below the surface. In some cases, copulation can occur on the surface at night.

As the eggs develop, they form a mass containing up to 300,000 eggs attached to the female's abdomen. She enters the water for the eggs to hatch. The crab larvae are microscopic and are part of the floating plankton found in tidal waters. The crab larvae undergo five molts, assuming their adult form in six to eight weeks. The newly molted fiddler is small and will still undergo several molts until it reaches its full size, depending on species, of about one or two inches.

Fiddler crabs are food for many species of wildlife: raccoons, herons, and above all, white ibis. White ibis will gather on mud flats in groups of fifty to a hundred and probe in the mud for fiddlers, one of their favorite foods.

Another small crab with equal-sized claws lives just above the high tide line. Because it resides on docks, it is called the wharf crab (*Sesarma cinereum*).

SNAILS, TERRAPINS & FILTER FEEDERS

The population of snails in the marsh may well exceed that of the fiddler crabs. Marsh periwinkles live on the cord grass itself: eating algae, other microscopic organisms or the grass tissue itself. Mud snails live on the muddy bottoms, exposed only during low tides. They eat detritus and microscopic organisms that live in the mud. Both of these snails are food for larger animals.

Although snakes will swim across tidal creeks to get to

islands, and alligators occasionally enter brackish water, the diamondback terrapin is the only reptile that exclusively lives in the salt marshes. So far as is known, it is the only species of turtle known to live and thrive in brackish water. The sea turtles remain in the very saline ocean water. Most of the terrapins' lives are spent in the marsh water. The females will grow to ten inches; males are rarely longer than five inches. They mate, in the water, in early spring.

The female crawls out of the water above the high tide line to lay her eggs. In late spring or early summer, this is one of the rare times she leaves the water. She lays four to eighteen eggs, which she buries in the sand. In two to four months, the inch-long hatchlings emerge and enter the nearest water. The male reaches maturity in three years, whereas, the female reaches maturity in six to seven years.

How long terrapins live is uncertain, but estimates vary from twenty to forty years. Terrapins usually live out their lives in the same creek. The terrapins eat fish, crustaceans, and mollusks, especially snails and fiddler crabs. They hibernate in the mud during cold weather.

The terrapins were once extensively hunted for food in the United States. Terrapin soup was a popular gourmet item on the East Coast. In the 1920s, about 35,000 terrapins per year were exported from Savannah, Georgia. Now the terrapins enjoy legal protection, but other threats to them exist. Creekside development eliminates the sandy areas where the terrapins lay their eggs. Automobiles hit terrapins crossing roads to lay eggs. A major threat is the crab trap. When terrapins enter the crab traps, they cannot escape and they drown. Research is currently being conducted to develop a crab trap that would exclude the terrapin. The population of terrapins in our coastal marsh varies from place to place. In some locales, they are abundant. In other locales, few or none exist.

Most of the salt marsh biomass resides in the tidal waters itself. The base of the marsh food chain is plankton: a floating mass of organisms, mostly microscopic, including algae, bacteria, protozoa, copepodes, and the larvae of mollusks and crustaceans, such as crab, shrimp, and barnacles, as well as minute larvae of fish. The filter feeders, such as oysters and mussels, feed directly on plankton, which they sieve from the water. The oyster is a colonial bivalve, adhering to one another to form large "reefs" on the creek bottom or dock posts.

The mussel is a single organism, although they may grow in clusters that live in the mud beneath the cord grass. They gape open to feed during high tide and close their shells tightly during low tide.

SHRIMP, CRABS & FISH

The small grass shrimp spend their entire lives in the tidal creek waters. The larvae of other crustaceans, *Penaeus* shrimp (the edible kind), blue crab, and stone crab, move into the tidal creeks as part of the plankton. Shrimp and crabs enter the tidal creeks to mature, because the young require reduced salinity to grow and flourish. The salinity of the coast marshes is a gradient, ranging from the freshwater of the rivers that flow into the marsh to the high salinity (thirty-five percent) of the ocean water.

During times of drought, when less fresh water flows into the salt marsh, the populations of crab and shrimp are affected. An infectious dinoflagelate protozoan, known as *Hematodidum*, flourishes during periods of high salinity. This protozoan infects the blood system of crabs. During a draught, the population of crabs is reduced by *Hermatodium* infections. The health of our salt marshes is dependent upon a reservoir of fresh water stored in the upriver marshes and swamps.

Three small species of minnow are abundant in the salt marsh: the mummichog, silversides, and the striped killifish. All three are predators that eat small organisms; in turn, they are prey of larger fish and birds. These minnow schools will ruffle the surface of the tidal matters as they feed. Mummichogs and killifish are the only fish that spend their entire lives in the tidal creeks, including waters only a few inches deep. Many fish swim up the creeks to feed, and many larval forms move into the tidal creeks to grow to maturity, including Penaeus shrimp, blue crabs, red drum, sea trout, spot, and croaker; in other words, they use the tidal creeks as nursery grounds.

Flounder, sting rays, even sharks swim into the creeks to feed. Hundreds of species of fish feed in the tidal creeks. Dolphins follow the fish up the creek. Dolphins will chase fish up onto exposed mud banks, rolling over and gobbling up the stranded fish.

One species of fish that all marsh observers notice is the mullet because they leap out of the water. Why mullet leap is still uncertain, but the imaginative human observer wonders if they enjoy their leaps toward the sky. Mullet are bottom feeders and are rarely caught with hook and line. They are harvested with nets.

SPARTINA MARSHES:
FINAL THOUGHTS

Spartina salt marshes extend along the Atlantic Coast from New England to northern Florida and along the northern coast of the Gulf of Mexico. Similar ecosystems with related species of *Spartina* are found on the West Coast of our continent and the West Coast of

Europe. The most extensive expanses of *Spartina* salt marsh exist on the coast of Georgia and South Carolina. These coastal marshes are the result of the interaction of the tidal extremes (six to nine feet) of the Southeast Bight and many rivers that flow from the mountains and piedmont, across the Coastal Plain to the sea.

Though this book is organized into chapters descnbing distinct ecosystems, most habitats are not distinct units, like bricks in a building, but a continuum blending from one to another. The fresh water marshes upriver blend into the brackish water marshes, then into the more saline marshes near the ocean. Some plant species are adapted to survive in brackish waters, such as the giant millet or foxtail (*Setaria magna*) and the big cord grass (*Spartina cyanosuroides*). These grasses can grow over ten feet high and are commonly found in the transition area between fresh and saltwater marshes.

The organisms that are successful in the coastal marshes have to be adapted to survive the variable salinity levels of the marsh waters. For example, a heavy rain can dilute the very saline ocean waters.

The seasonal color changes of the salt marsh are beautiful to observe. In the late summer, the marshes are bright green. In the early fall, salt marshes are topped with a white frosting as the cord grass flowers. The flowers mature into straw-gold seeds, then the grass blades begin to die back. First, the blade tips turn gold, and then the color extends gradually toward the base of the plant. By midwinter, the marsh shines straw-gold. By late winter, the cord grass becomes brown, but by that time new green blades are springing forth from the base of the cord grass, reaching maturity by spring. The spring marsh is a grizzled mixture of green and brown. The dead brown stalks will be stripped away by the tides, but most of the summer is needed for the job to be completed. Initially, the greening of the marsh occurs at the banks of the tidal creeks, then the green extends back to the high marsh. The marsh is not fully green until late summer when the cycle begins anew. The dead stalks form mats, known as wrack, that float on the tide until they decay into detritus. Some of the wrack ends up on the beaches.

The early European settlers on the Southeast Coast avoided the coastal marshes and cleared and built on the higher ground; thus, the marshes survived. Modern technology could destroy the marshes. Thanks to the development of conservation consciousness among Americans, the coastal marshes are now protected by law. The coastal salt marshes are unique, diverse, productive, and beautiful. We can rejoice in their survival and protection.

Salt Marsh

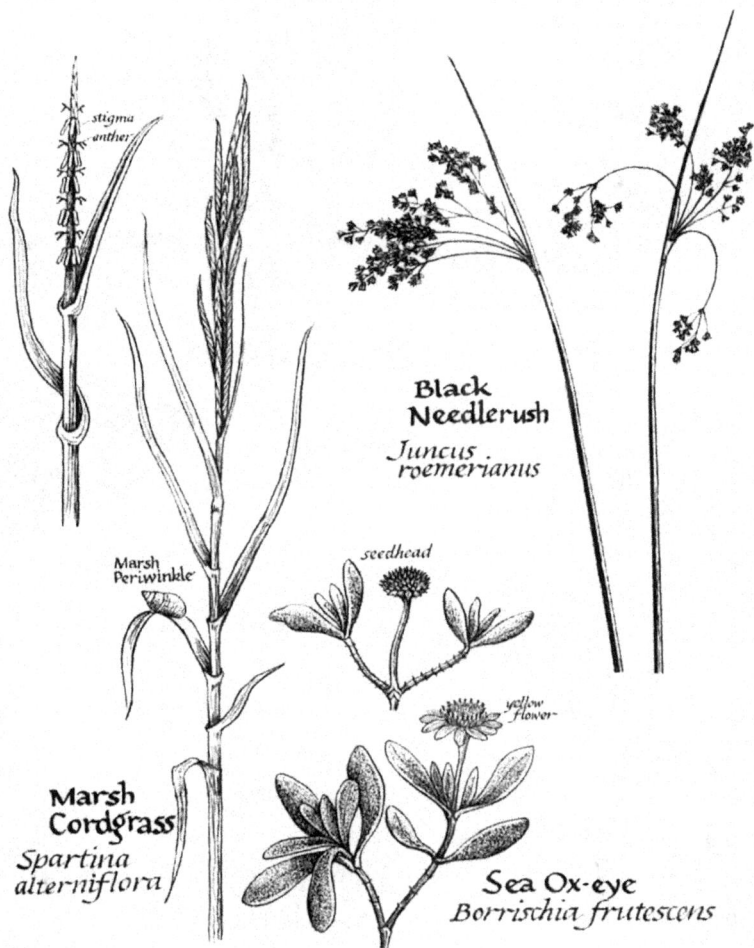

stigma
anther

Black
Needlerush
*Juncus
roemerianus*

Marsh
Periwinkle

seedhead

Marsh
Cordgrass
*Spartina
alterniflora*

yellow
flower

Sea Ox-eye
Borrischia frutescens

Saltmarsh Plants

Saltwort
Batis maritima

Salicornia
Glasswort or
Pickleweed

Marsh Succulents

Marsh
Elder
Iva
frutescens

Groundsel Tree or
Cottonbush
Baccharis halimifolia

Marsh Edge Plants

Big Cordgrass
*Spartina
cyanosuroides*

Giant Foxtail/Millet
Setaria magna

Brackish Water Plants

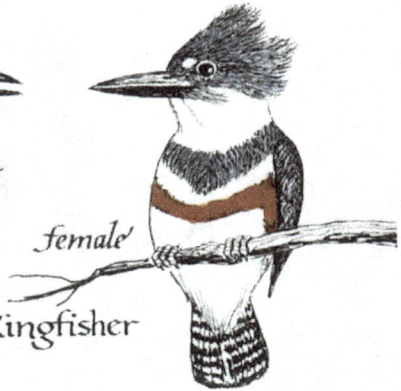

male

female

Belted Kingfisher

Red-winged Blackbird

Clapper Rail

male

young
4 in.

female

adult
14-15 in.

Marsh Birds

Marsh
Wrens
with nest

orange face
Sharp-
tailed
Sparrow

Seaside
Sparrow

Savannah
Sparrow

Otter

otter track

otter & mink scats have fish scales

mink track

Mink

Marsh Rice Rat

Marsh Rabbit

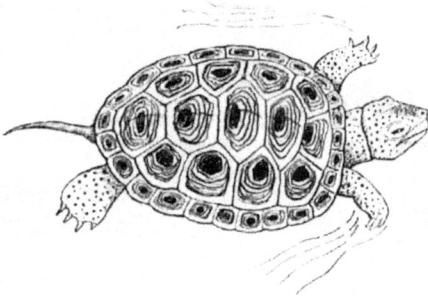

Diamondback Terrapin

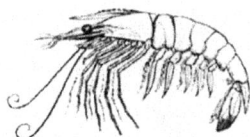

Penaeus shrimp

male

female

Fiddler Crabs
Uca spp

Wharf crab
Sesarma cinereum

Blue Crab
Callinectes sapinus

Stone Crab
Menippe mercenaria

Ribbed Mussel
Glukensia demissa

Oyster Reef
Crossostreya virginica

Salt Marsh Invertebrates

Fiddler Crabs

Sand Fiddler *Uca pugilator*

Mud Fiddler *Uca pugnax*

Brackish *or* Red-jointed Fiddler *Uca minax*

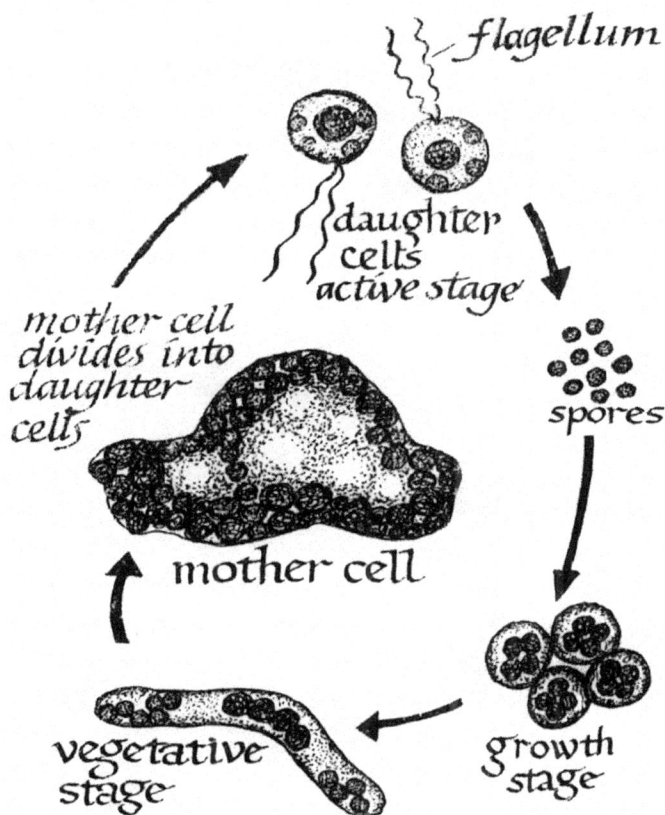

Life Cycle of *Hematodidium*
Dinoflagelate protozoan infecting
Crabs

Mullet
Mugil cephalus

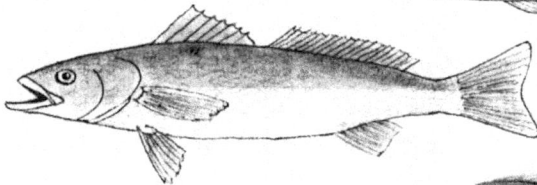

Seatrout or
Weakfish
Cynoscion spp

Flounder
Paralichthys spp.

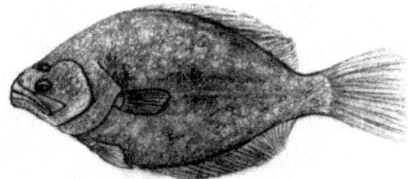

Croaker
*Micropogonias
undulatus*

Red Drum
Sciaenops ocellatus

Mum-
michog
*Fundulus
heteroclitus*

Silverside
Menidia spp.

Striped Killifish
Fundulus majolis

Small Marsh Fish
5 to 7 inches

WADING BIRDS

The wading bird group (*Ciconiformes*) includes heron, ibis, storks, and spoonbills. They are all long-legged, long-necked birds adapted for catching prey; they mostly reside in wetlands, both salt-water and freshwater, but their feeding habits vary.

The herons are stalkers: they hunt visually and capture prey with the spear-like bills. Their long necks enable them to strike quickly like a snake. The large herons, like the great blue heron and great egret, wait patiently, standing in shallow water, poised to strike when the prey comes close. Small herons, especially the snowy egret, will sometimes dash about with open wings and strike rapidly, often stirring the water with their feet. The small green heron may fish while standing on the bank beside the water or from floating docks. Herons usually prey upon fish, crustaceans, frogs, or insects. The large herons may capture snakes, small mammals, or small birds.

An interesting adaptation of the heron's eyes is that while resting or perching, the eyes face outward to the side, giving the heron vision behind. This type of vision is good for observing preda-tors sneaking up from behind. When they stalk prey, they rotate their eyes forward, providing binocular vision, which gives the heron better three-dimensional perception. Binocular vision enables the heron to sight and catch their prey with greater accuracy. Herons usually hunt alone. If the food is abundant, they may feed in groups and sometimes with other species. But great blue herons or great egrets will chase others from their hunting territory. The great blue typically hunts alone and behaves aggressively toward its own kind. The great blue heron can be observed fishing alongside a great or snowy egret or perhaps a tricolored heron.

The primary diet of the cattle egrets includes insects. These birds feed in open fields with cattle or the grassy rights of ways beside roads. This egret is very social and often feeds in groups. The cattle egret is a recent arrival from Africa, showing up in Brazil in the 1930s. Now it is quite abundant in the United States.

Ibises probe shallow water with their long, curved bills, seeking crustaceans like small crabs and crayfish or small fish. They also probe in grassy areas, sticking their long beaks into the ground up to the base of the bill, seeking underground insects. Ibis usually feed together in large flocks. In the coastal marshes, the white ibises gather on mud flats to eat fiddler crabs.

The wood stork feeds tactilely in shallow water, swaying their heads slowly back and forth with open beaks immersed in the water. When the beak encounters prey, it automatically snaps shut. While feeding. storks will stir the water with their feet. Although storks will feed alone, they prefer to feed in groups. Their prey includes small fish and crustacean. Storks feed on dead fish, too, pulling pieces of flesh off the carcass.

Wading birds usually nest communally in large flocks, often hundreds of birds of mixed species. Anhingas frequently nest among the wading birds. The nests are built of sticks in shrubs or trees, preferably surrounded by alligator-infested ponds. The alligators deter raccoons from invading the nests.

Storks and great blue herons prefer tall trees. The great blue may build solitary nests or nest communally in small groups of ten to twelve. The majority of the communal heronries are close to the coast. Green herons, however, build solitary nests in large trees, like oaks. Large birds, such as storks and great blue herons need open space access to their large nests. Small green herons easily negotiate through heavy foliage. Green herons will nest in backyard trees in inhabited areas. Human neighbors will deter predators, such as hawks.

Most waders usually raise two to four young per year. Ibis and stork nests are built close to each other. Herons and egrets space out their nests beyond the stabbing distance of their neighbor. Although herons nest colonially, they are territorial in the immediate vicinity of their nest. Herons and egrets have nuptial plumes on their backs which they erect during courting ritual or aggressive displays. These plumes, known as aigrettes, nearly led to the extinction of egrets. In the nineteenth and early twentieth century, the birds were hunted for the aigrettes which were used on ladies' hats. The market hunters invaded the rookeries, shot the nesting birds, stripped off the desired feathers, and discarded the carcasses. The population of the plumed creatures plummeted.

After federal protection was established in 1918, the population of herons and egrets rebounded. As long as we protect their habitats, especially the breeding locales, these birds should do fine. The egrets and the great blue herons are the most abundant herons in the Southeast, but the tricolored heron (three colors: blue-purple body, white belly, and lavender back) often feeds or nests with the egrets. The tricolored is fairly common but not as numerous as the egrets. The little blue heron population is smaller than that of other herons. Although this heron can be observed in the coastal salt marsh, its preferred habitat is wooded swamps. During its first year, this heron is white with a blue bill. For it to reach its adult plumage, a dark purple, it takes three years. Its transition plumage is white with blue splotches scattered over its body.

The night herons (black-crowned and yellow-crowned) primarily feed at night, resting quietly in trees during the day. These herons are more solitary than the other herons, and their preferred habitats are wooded swamps.

American and least bitterns prefer freshwater marshes. They nest in the marsh vegetation just above high water line.

Before 1960. no white ibis lived on the Georgia Coast; their range was restricted to South Florida and South America. Since that time. they have extended their range north and are now abundant up to Virginia. The glossy ibis, originally from Africa, has only a few nesting locales in the Southeast. Compared to the white ibis. its population is small.

The wood storks are abundant in South America, but this species is classified as endangered in the United States. The principle breeding locale in the United States is Florida. Due to the loss of wet-lands because of agricultural development and changing hydrologic conditions, many storks moved north to breed. Florida still has 7.000 breeding pairs; Georgia now has 1,600 pairs. and South Carolina 2,000 pairs. The wood stork population is doing well in the United States.

Most waders feed their young regurgitated food directly into their open mouths. Storks regurgitate the food onto the bottom of the nest, then the young gobble it. Except for bill-clapping greetings, the adults are silent. Their young are noisy with a continuous din of harsh nasal squawks. Before the bills grow long. the young ibis take the regurgitated food directly from the parents. As the young grow and their bills assume the long, sickle shape, the adults regurgitate onto the bottom of nests for their young to feed.

The wading birds are large and spectacular. In the past, the populations of these birds declined due to hunting. The birds themselves and their feeding grounds, the coastal marshes, are now protected. The wading birds usually nest on trees surrounded by freshwater ponds with alligators. lf we protect these nesting sites, we will continue to have a healthy and growing population of these beautiful birds.

Ibis

Stork

Storks & Ibis fly with necks
outstretched. Herons
usually fold their necks.

Heron

2 feet
high

yellow
bill

blue
bill

yellow
feet

yellow
legs

yellow
-green
legs

Snowy
Egret

Cattle
Egret

Little
Blue Heron
immature

Tricolored
Heron
purple-blue
white belly

3½ to
4 feet
high

yellow
-bill

Wood Storks

Great
Blue Heron

Great Egret

Wading Birds

White Ibis   *2 feet tall*   Glossy Ibis

Little Blue
Heron

American
Bittern

Yellow-crowned
Night Heron

immature Black
Crowned
Night
Heron

Small
Herons

Green Heron
19 inches

Least
Bittern
13 inches

Wading Birds

Wood Storks
with young

nuptial plumes

Great
Egret
with young

Snowy
Egret

displaying

Wading Birds

FRESHWATER MARSHES

Southeastern United States has many rivers that flow from the Appalachian Mountains to the coast where they feed into the coastal saltwater marshes. As the rivers approach the ocean, their waters blend with the saline ocean water and produce a gradient from the fresh water upriver, through multiple degrees of brackishness to the high salinity of the ocean. In many cases, these rivers feed into freshwater marshes that spread out from the river banks. These alluvial freshwater marshes, associated with rivers, are still tidal; high tides will push the waters upriver to be released as the tides recede. Thus, the alluvial freshwater marshes have a tidal pulse similar to the coastal salt marshes. Tidal amplitudes up to seven and a half feet flood thousands of acres of these freshwater marshes.

With fresh water, plants and animals do not have the problem of excreting salt. The constant exchange of nutrients drives this ecosystem's productivity.

The plants of the salt marsh differ from those of the freshwater marsh. A handful of plant species grow in the salt marsh; the dominant plant is the marsh cord grass (*Spartina alterniflora*) which covers over seventy-three percent of the salt marsh. By contrast, the freshwater marshes have over a hundred species of plants, including cattails, numerous grasses, sedges and rushes, and many plants with beautiful flowers, such as water lilies, pond lilies, lotuses, wild iris, pickerelweed, and arums. The salt marsh cord grass will grow in fresh water, but it cannot compete with the freshwater plants. The detritus from the freshwater plants, many of which are annuals, is easily broken down and used by the biotic community.

The giant cutgrass (*Zizaniopsis miliacea)* and cattails (*Typha* spp.) are the most abundant grass-like plants in the freshwater marsh. Scattered among these plants are wild rice (*Zizania aquatica*), several species of wild millet or water grass (*Echinochloa* spp.) and switch grasses (*Panicum* spp.). Open areas of deeper water may be covered with expanses of white water lilies (*Nymphaea adorata*) paved with flat round leaves that float on the surface and white, multi-petalled flowers that stand erect above the water. At scattered locales through the marsh are two water lily relatives, the pond lily or spadderdock (*Nuphar advena*) that has a compact yellow flower, and the spectacular American lotus (*Nelumbo lutea*). The lotus has large circular leaves standing erect on their stems above the water and large, multi-petalled, yellow-cream flowers. Both of these "lilies" grow in clusters in deeper water.

The distribution of plants in the freshwater marsh depends

83

on water depth. The grass-like plants grow in shallow water; the water lilies grow in deeper water. In the intermediate depth water are dense masses of lush, flowering plants with lance-shaped, arrow-shaped, or heart- shaped leaves: several species of *Sagittaria*, pickerelweed (*Pontederia cordata*), golden club (*Orontium aquaticum*) and arrow-arum (*Peltandra virginica*).

Several other flowers can be found in the intermediate zone. The swamp rose mallow (*Hibiscus moscheutos*) grows up to three feet tall and bears a large white flower with a red center, which blooms through most of the summer. The blue flag iris (*Iris versicolor*), which resembles the garden iris, blooms in spring (April to May); the scarlet lobelia (*Lobelia cardinalis*) blooms in late summer (July to October). The white spiderlily (*Hymenocallis crassifoliay*) blooms from May through June. The bladderpod (*Utricularia* spp.) is a floating plant and can be found on open water. Bur marigolds (*Bidens laevis*) bloom in August and September.

Two exotics introduced from South America form dense mats: water primrose (*Ludwigia uraguayensis*); with bright yellow flowers blooming through the summer, and alligator weed (*Alternathera philoxeroides*). The alligator weed, considered a nuisance invader, bears a small white bundle of flowers vaguely resembling a clover bloom.

An invasive grass introduced from Europe, common reed (*Phragmites australis*), can grow to ten feet. Some marsh areas in North Carolina have been completely taken over by common reed.

Most marshes have many species of grass-like rushes and sedges. Rushes (*Juncus* spp.) are characterized by a tall, thin spike, which can be soft or hard with a sharp point. The flowers and seeds dangle from this tall spike.

Sedges are a large and diverse family, but they have characteristics in common. The stem nodes are triangular in cross section, the leaves of which are three-ranked and the fruit is a nutlet rather than a grain, as in grasses. The common sedges are *Cypressus* and *Carex* sedges, bulrushes (*Scirpus* spp.), spike rushes (*Eleocharis* spp.) and beak-rushes (*Rhynchosporas*). The white-topped sedge (*Dichromena latifolia*) is the only one with a showy flower. Saw grass (*Cladium jamaciensis*) is a sedge, not a grass. Although the dominant plant in the Everglade prairies, it is only an occasional plant in the marshes of Georgia and Carolina.

Some plants grow at the marsh edges, such as two members of the parsley family: water hemlock (*Circuta maculata*), related to poison hemlock, and water parsnip (*Sium suave*). Both species have pinnately compound leaves and flat clusters of small white flowers, like their relative, Queen Anne's lace. The buttonbush (*Cephalanthus occidentalis*) will grow to ten feet high and, through the summer, bears globular "buttons" consisting of clusters of small white flowers.

The salt marsh has one showy flower, sea oxeye, but the fresh water marsh has many species of showy flowers of diverse shapes, sizes, and colors. Through spring and summer, the freshwater marsh is a beautiful flower garden.

Much of the same wildlife occupies both salt and freshwater marshes: herons, egrets, storks, and ibis, as well as otter, mink and raccoon. Many species of wildlife, birds, reptiles, amphibians, and fish only occupy freshwater marshes. Other species only occupy salt marshes.

Freshwater marshes provide important habitat for migrating songbirds and wintering waterfowl, especially the dabbling ducks, such as mallard, teal, pintail, widgeon, and shovellers. The dabbling ducks are vegetarians. The freshwater marshes provide plenty of food for them; the salt marsh does not. Dabbling ducks also consume underwater insects that are abundant in the detritus of freshwater annual plants. These insects will not survive in salt water.

The wintering ducks that inhabit the salt marsh are the mergansers (fish eaters) and bay ducks such as scaup and bufflehead which eat crustaceans, mollusks, and salt water algae. The dabbling ducks are rare visitors to the salt marsh. The wood duck, another freshwater species is our only summer species; they breed in hollow trees ... or bird boxes.

Most marshes have rails. The salt marshes are the exclusive home of the clapper rail, known locally as a marsh hen. The freshwater marshes are home to a similar species known as the king rail. In brackish marshes, where salt and fresh water meet, these two rails will hybridize. For this reason, some biologists consider them to be ecological races of the same species.

The freshwater marshes are home to several species of rails, the most conspicuous being the similar-appearing moorhens, coots, and purple gallinules. Most rails are secretive, furtively running or walking through the marsh grass. Moorhens, coots, and gallinules swim in the open water like ducks. The long-toed purple gallinule, a colorful species sporting a red bill with blue and purple plumage, will walk over lily pads with high steps.

Two species of rails are elusive and hard to see. They usually hide in the grass. The Virginia rail resembles the king rail, but is smaller (nine and a half inches) as opposed to the king rail's fifteen inches. The black-masked sora is also small (eight and three-quarters inches).

Two species of heron prefer freshwater: the American bittern and the least bittern, our smallest heron. Both are chunky brownish birds that hide in the marsh grass.

Much admired by visitors among freshwater or brackish water birds is the anhinga, a cousin of the cormorant. Like the cormorant, the anhinga perches on trees or stumps, spreading its wings to dry after it emerges from under water. It is the only bird I know that will catch a fish by spearing it. It has a sharply pointed bill unlike the cormorant, which has a hook at the end of its beak. The anhinga has a long tail, which it can spread, leading to another common name: the water turkey. It will often swim under water with only its long neck and head exposed, suggesting another name: snake bird. This bird is very much at home under the water but it is equally at home high in the sky. They soar and circle like vultures. Related species live in Africa and Asia where they are known as darters. Both anhingas and cormorants have small gular pouches at their throats. They happen to be distantly related to pelicans.

Cormorants are equally at home in salt or fresh water, but the anhinga prefers fresh water. One colorful warbler, the common yellowthroat, nests in low shrubs in freshwater marshes. The swamp sparrow is a winter visitor to the southeastern freshwater marshes.

One terrapin, the Carolina diamondback, lives in brackish marshes, but the freshwater marsh has several cooters, sliders, mud turtles, soft-shelled turtles, and snapping turtles. The marsh has snakes, including the poisonous water moccasin and the common water snake, and, of course, alligators. Adult alligators can live in salt water, but the young need fresh water to survive and grow.

The female alligator builds a nest of grass and other vegetation into which she lays her eggs. The decaying vegetation provides the heat to incubate the eggs. She guards the nest and the hatched young until they are big enough to function on their own. An adult alligator is a formidable animal, but the young are vulnerable to predation from storks, herons, raccoons, and male alligators.

Amphibians, which cannot survive salt water, flourish in freshwater marshes, including several species of salamanders and frogs, such as the bullfrog and leopard frog.

Many of these freshwater marshes were once used as rice plantations. Now they have reverted to natural marshes, but the dikes and sluice gates remain. Harbor development has resulted in upriver incursion of salt water. The old dikes have been used to maintain the fresh water in these marshes. Proscribed fire, in the fall and February, is used as a management technique in these former

rice plantations. Fire removes dead vegetation, allows for renewed
vigorous growth in the spring, and promotes greater plant diversity.
Managers of freshwater marshes often take steps to control invasive
plants, such as cattails, and encourage growth of plants like millet
and wild rice that are useful as food for ducks and other wildlife.

Freshwater Marsh

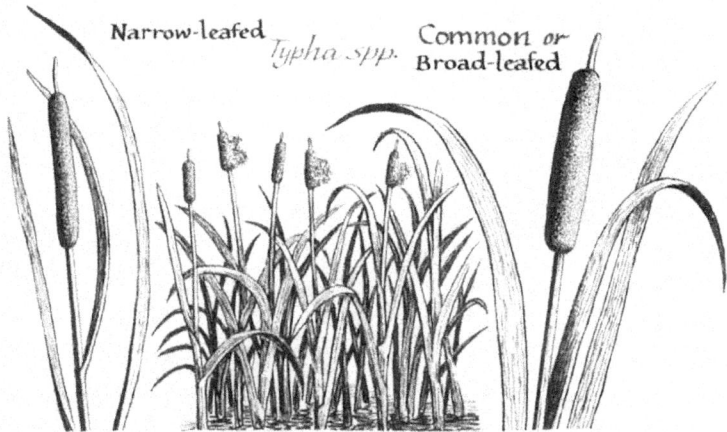

Narrow-leafed *Typha spp.* Common or Broad-leafed

Cattails

Wild Rice
Zizania aquatica

Giant Cutgrass or
Southern Wild Rice
Zizaniopsis milacea

Arrow-Arum
Peltandra spp.

Golden Club
*Orontium
aquaticum*

Arum Family

Pickerelweed
*Pontederia
cordata*

Spider Lily
*Hymenocallis
caroliniana*

88

Spikerush
Eleocharis spp.

White-topped Sedge
Dichromena latifolia

Cyperus Sedge

Carex Sedge

Sedges

Bladderpod
Utricularia spp.

Swamp Rose Mallow
*Hibiscus
moscheutos*

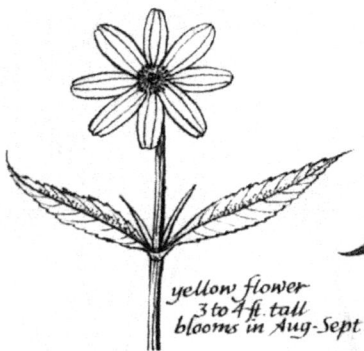

yellow flower
3 to 4 ft. tall
blooms in Aug-Sept.

Bur-Marigold
Bidens laevis

Lizard's Tail
Saururus cernuus

Buttonbush
Cephalanthus occidentalis

Water Swart Weed

Polygonum punctatum

Blue Flag Iris
Iris versicolor

White Water Lily
Nymphaea odorata

American Lotus
Nelumbo liltea

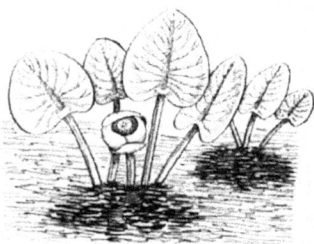

Spadderdock or Pond Lily
Nuphar advena

Broad-leaved
Sagittaria latifolia

Cardinal
Flower or
Scarlet
Lobelia
Lobelia cardinalis

Narrow-leaved
Sagittaria lancifolia

Arrowhead, Duck-potato
or *Sagittaria*

Beak-
rush

Rhynchosporas spp.

Marsh Bullrush
*Scirpus
cyperinus*

Sedges

Rush
Juncus spp.

Switch Grass
Panicum spp

Wild Millet or
Water grass
*Echinochloa
ssp.*

Water Primrose
Ludwigia
uraguayensis

Alligator Weed
Alternathera philoxeroides

Common Reed
Phragmites australis
up to 10 feet tall

Exotic Invasive Marsh
Plants

Alligator

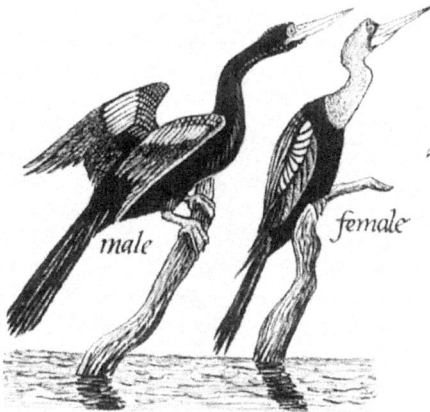

male

female

Anhinga

Double Crested
Cormorant

Bufflehead

Ruddy Duck

Scaup

Lesser Scaup

Greater Scaup

female resembles female scaup.

Canvasback

Redhead

Ring-necked Duck

Hooded Merganser

Red-Breasted Merganser

Sora

King
Rail

King Rail (15 in.) is russet
Clapper Rail is gray-brown

Moorhen

Coot

Purple
Gallinule

Pied-billed Grebe

Yellowthroat
*female has yellow
throat but no mask*

Swamp
Sparrow

Wood Duck
Summer duck

Mallard

Female is mottled brown but has a long neck & tail

Pintail

Shoveller

Blue-winged Teal

Green-winged Teal

female has a pink body & gray head

Widgeon

Gadwall

Freshwater Wetlands

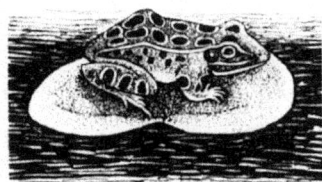

Leopard Frog
Rana utricularia

Bullfrog
Rana catesbeiana

Spring Peeper
Pseudacris crucifer

Cricket Frog
Acris gryllus

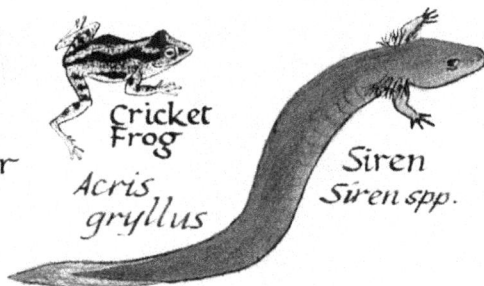

Siren
Siren spp.

Water Snake
Nerodia spp.

Cottonmouth or Water Moccasin
Agkistrodon piscivorus

Freshwater Turtles

Soft-shelled Turtle
Apalone spinifera

Yellow-bellied Slider
Trachemys scripta

Mud Turtle
Kinasternon spp

Musk Turtle
Stenotherus spp.

Cooter
Pseudemys spp.

Snapping Turtle
Chelydra serpentina

FRESHWATER SWAMPS

A swamp is a wetland with trees and shrubs. Most swamps in the Southeast are alluvial, that is they are associated with rivers or their tributaries. The large swamps, like the Okefenokee or Great Dismal Swamp are backwater swamps, spreading out over vast expanses of lowland. They are watersheds, giving rise to rivers.

CYPRESS-TUPELO SWAMPS

The dominant trees that grow in the swamp waters are bald cypresses (*Taxodium distichum*) and water tupelo (*Nyssa aquatica*). The bald cypress is found in the Coastal Plains ranging from south Virginia to Florida, west to east Texas, and in the Mississippi Valley up to the southern tips of Illinois and Indiana.

Water tupelo has a similar range, but it is absent from South Georgia and Florida. Cypress and water tupelo have swollen buttresses at their bases. Bald cypress is not a true cypress but a member of the *Taxodium* family which includes the sequoias. Junipers are in the true Cypress family. The needles and cones of the bald cypress are virtually identical with those of the coast redwood (*Sequoia sempervirens*) of California. The coast redwood is evergreen, whereas the cypress is deciduous. Cypress needles turn red-brown in the fall and are shed through the winter. Like the coast redwood, the bald cypress is long-lived (up to 2,000 years) and can become a large tree with a diameter of five feet or more. Because the wood of the cypress was desirable, the only ancient cypress remaining is found in the more inaccessible reaches of large swamps. Cypress is rarely lumbered today and many second-growth cypresses are reaching mature sizes in protected areas.

William Bartram, the great botanist-explorer, described cypresses in evocative terms on his travels through Georgia and the Carolinas in 1791:

On my doubling a long point of land. the river appeared surprisingly widened, forming a large bay, of an oval form, and several miles in extent. On the West side it was bordered round with low marshes, and invested with a swamp of Cypress, the trees so lofty, as to preclude the sight of the highland forests beyond them; and these trees, having flat tops, and all of equal height, seemed to be a green plain, lifted up and supported upon columns in the air, round the West side of the bay.

The Cypressus disticha stands in the first order of North American trees. Its majestic stature is surprising; and on approaching it, we are struck with

101

a kind of awe, at beholding the stateliness of the trunk, lifting its cumbrous top towards the skies, and casting a wide shade upon the ground, as a dark intervening cloud, which, for a time, excludes the rays of the sun. The delicacy of its colour and texture of its leaves exceed every thing in vegetation. It generally grows in the water, or in low flat lands, near the banks of great rivers and lakes, that are covered, great part of the year, with two or three feet depth of water; and that part of the trunk which is subject to be under water, and four or five feet higher up, is greatly enlarged by prodigious buttresses, or pilasters, which, in full grown trees, project out on every side, to such a distance, that several men might easily hide themselves in the hollows between. Each pilaster terminates under ground, in a very large, strong, serpentine root, which strikes off, and branches every way, just under the surface of the earth: and from these roots grow woody cones, called cypress knees, four, five, and six inches high, and from six to eighteen inches and two feet in diameter at their bases. The large ones are hollow, and serve very well for beehives; a small space of tree itself is hollow, nearly as high as the buttresses already mentioned. From this place, the tree, as it were, takes another beginning, forming a grand straight column eighty or ninety feet high, when it divides every way around into an extensive flat horizontal top, like an umbrella, where eagles have their secure nests, and cranes and storks their temporary resting-places; and what adds to the magnificence of their appearance is the streamers of long moss that hang from the lofty limbs and float in the winds. This is their majestic appearance when standing alone, in large rice plantations, or thinly planted on the banks of great rivers.

Parroquets are commonly seen hovering and fluttering on their tops: they delight to shell the balls, its seed being their favorite food.

The colorful Carolina parroquet loved to eat the cypress seed and frequented the cypress forests. Unfortunately, the parroquet, once common throughout the Southeast, is extinct. The Carolina parroquet was last observed in the Everglades in 1920.

Spanish moss (*Tillandsia usneiodes*) survives on moisture in the air. Most swamp air provides perfect conditions for this airplant which will grow on the branches of any swamp tree. On higher, dry land, Spanish moss is limited to trees that exude water vapor, such as the live oak.

Water tupelo is a deciduous tree that bears purple berries. a close relative of the upland tree known as blackgum or black tupelo (*Nyssa sylvatica*).

The fruit of the water tupelo and the cones of the cypress float on water until they settle on soil and germinate. The water level in the alluvial swamps fluctuates according to the rainfall. During dry seasons, the swamp bottom is muddy soil with layers of leaf litter. The rust- red shallow creek winds its sinuous way through the muddy flats and ridges. During wet seasons, it inundates the entire swamp.

Single isolated cypresses or tupelos can be found scattered through the expanses of grassy freshwater marshes. Marsh plants such as water lilies, iris, and golden club border the creeks that wend their way through cypress-tupelo swamps.

Many other trees and shrubs are associated with swamps. Some grow adjacent to the rivers and are subject to periodic inundation. As we move away from the river's edge, a gradient occurs of moist to dryer soils and of trees that love moist soils.

Red maple (*Acer rubrum*), willow (*Salix*), hornbeam or ironwood (*Carpinus caroliniana)* are abundant on the rivers' edges. These are small trees. Several species of oaks prefer swampy areas: swamp laurel oak (*Quercus laurifolia*), swamp chestnut oak (*Q michauxii*) and willow oak (*Q phellos*). The water oak (*Q nige*r) grows in a variety of soil types, but it is often abundant adjacent to swamps.

The sweetgum (*Liquidambar styraciflua*) is ubiquitous in the Southeast, but it reaches its largest size on moist alluvial soils.

Other trees that grow in or adjacent to swamps are slippery elm (*Ulmus rubra*), witch hazel (*Hamemalis virginiana*), water hickory (*Carya aquatica*), tag alder (*Aldus serrulata*), Carolina ash (*Fraxinus caroliniana*), and pond pine (*Pinus serotina*). The Ogeechee lime or tupelo (*Nyssa ogeche*) is a small swamp tree in coastal Georgia and north Florida. Its fruit is sour like a lime.

Two small trees, known as bays that bear large white flowers, are restricted to areas with moist soils: loblolly bay (*Gordonia lasianthus*) and sweet bay or swamp bay magnolia (*Magnolia virginia*). Both are evergreen with large leaves. Gordonia's leaves have fine teeth on its edge, whereas the edges on the Magnolia's leaves are smooth (entire). The Gordonia flowers have five petals; the bay magnolia has six to fourteen petals similar to its larger relative, the southern magnolia (*Magnolia grandiflora*). Both magnolias bear cones with large bright red seeds.

Immediately adjacent to the swamp rivers, areas which are frequently inundated with water, the trees and shrubs are spaced out. In low water, the soil is exposed mud or leaf litter. In the land surrounding the swamps, areas of wet soil which flood occasionally, the understory is a lush growth of herbs, ferns, vines, *Smilax*, and shrubs, many of which are evergreen.

The shrubs include blueberries (*Vaccinium* spp.), a holly-gallberry (*Ilex glabra*), fetterbush or hurrah bush (*Lyonia lucida*), sweet pepperbush (*Clethra alnifolia*), and titi (*Cyrilla racimiflora*). The titi may be either a shrub or small tree.

The wildlife of swamps, especially birds, is similar to what you find in other freshwater wetlands: snakes, turtles, frogs, alligators, mink, and otter, and herons, egrets, storks and ibis. The large wading birds nest atop the tall cypress and tupelo. These trees in the swamp water provide an advantage to the nesting birds. Frequently, alligators lurk in the water below. Egg-stealing raccoons avoid waters where alligators reside.

The wood duck is the only duck that nests in the Southeast. For that reason, the wood duck is sometimes called the "summer duck." Most species of ducks are only winter visitors in the South. The wood duck prefers swamps because it builds its nest in hollow trees. The bright yellow prothonotary warbler is another swamp dweller that nests in hollow trees, in smaller holes than the wood duck. The Acadian flycatcher also nests in swamps.

Two hawks, the swallow-tailed kite and the Mississippi kite, nest in swamps, atop tall cypresses. The kites' prey are insects, catching them in flight over marshes or open fields. They nest and feed in groups. Both species will feed together, swooping to catch large insects in flight. Though they feed in open areas, they roost and nest in tall swamp trees. The swallow-tailed kite is a declining species. Preservation of cypress swamps where it nests is necessary for this kite's survival.

A swamp is a forest. Many forest birds live and nest in a swamp, including woodpeckers, such as the pileated woodpecker. The almost extinct ivory-billed woodpecker depended on old growth virgin swamps. This woodpecker declined as the virgin cypress swamps were cleared. It was thought to be extinct, but recently the ivorybill has been reported in some isolated swamps in Arkansas.

Traditionally, swamps are thought of as gloomy, dismal, horrible, and impenetrable, "a place fraught with difficulties." Yes, swamps are mysterious and sometimes difficult to enter and traverse, but they have their own beauty and unique plants and wildlife that make them interesting to explore and study.

OKEFENOKEE SWAMP

The Okefenokee Swamp is one of the largest freshwater wetlands in the United States, about 700 square miles. It is mixed habitat: twenty-one percent is marsh (known as "prairies"); twenty-nine percent, swamp forest (cypress swamp); thirty-four percent, swamp shrub; eight percent, upland islands; and seven percent, open water.

The wetlands are either tidal or alluvial (around a river). The Okefenokee Swamp is a backwater swamp, a flooded depression surrounded by higher ground. Although a few Okefenokee lakes have deeper water, up to ten feet, most of the swamp is no deeper than two feet. There is less flow in this swamp than river swamps, and organic matter gathers on the bottom to form peat. This organic matter releases tannic acid into the water, making it coffee-colored. The soil is quite acidic, affecting what can grow there. Some of the islands are floating mats of peat, which led to the Indian name of Okefenokee, which means "Land of the Trembling Earth." The rivers that feed the alluvial wetlands rise in the Appalachian Mountains and foothills and flow either east to the Atlantic Ocean or south to the Gulf of Mexico.

Okefenokee gives rise to two major rivers. The Suwannee flows southwest to the Gulf of Mexico. The St. Mary's flows primarily eastward to the border between Georgia and Florida.

Much of the flora and fauna of the Okefenokee is similar to the flora and fauna of the southeastern wetlands, but there are distinct differences.

The Okefenokee is subject to periodic fires which favor cypress and pine over hardwoods. The Okefenokee islands and surrounding uplands have forests similar to the Coastal Plain forests: mixed hardwoods and pine forests including the longleaf pine forest.

In alluvial marshes, cutgrass and cattails are dominant plants, but maidencane (*Panicum hemitomon*) is the dominant grass in the Okefenokee prairies. Other prairie and creek plants include sedges, water lilies, pond lilies, floating heart (*Nymphoides aquatica*), Golden club, *Peltandra* arums, pickerel weed, *Sagittaria*, iris and bladderwort. Spaghnum moss floats just below the surface throughout the swamp waters.

Carnivorous plants, including pitcher plants, sundews, and butter worts, grow in the boggy areas. Cypress groves and forests are common in the Okefenokee. The water tupelo (*Nyssa aquatica*) is absent from the Okefenokee, South Georgia, and Florida and is replaced by a subspecies of black gum known as swamp tupelo (*Nyssa sylvatica biflora*). Another Nyssa species, known as Ogeechee lime (*Nyssa ogeche*) is common in the Okefenokee. This is a shrub rather than a tree.

Shrubs and small trees grow in the swamp or the swamp edges. Hurrah bush (*Lyonia lucida*) is especially common, but a number of shrubs are common in the Okefenokee, many of which are common in any swamp edge in the Southeast: loblolly bay (*Gordonia*), swamp bay (*Magnolia virginiana*), titi (*Cyrilla racemiflora*), fetter bush (*Leucothoe racemosa*), pepperbush (*Clethra alnifolia*), blueberries

105

(*Vaccinium*) and gallberry (*Ilex glabra*).

Pine forests and sand ridge scrub oak forests are common upland Okefenokee forests.

The vertebrates in the Okefenokee are similar to other wetland and forest vertebrates throughout the Southeast (see other chapters in this field guide), but the black bear and alligator are common.

The Florida sandhill crane is resident in the Okefenokee. In the winter, migrating flocks of greater sandhill cranes join the resident cranes. The Florida sandhill crane is a non-migratory subspecies found in the Okefenokee south through Florida.

Swamps

Bald Cypress
Taxodium distichum

Water Tupelo
Nyssa aquatica

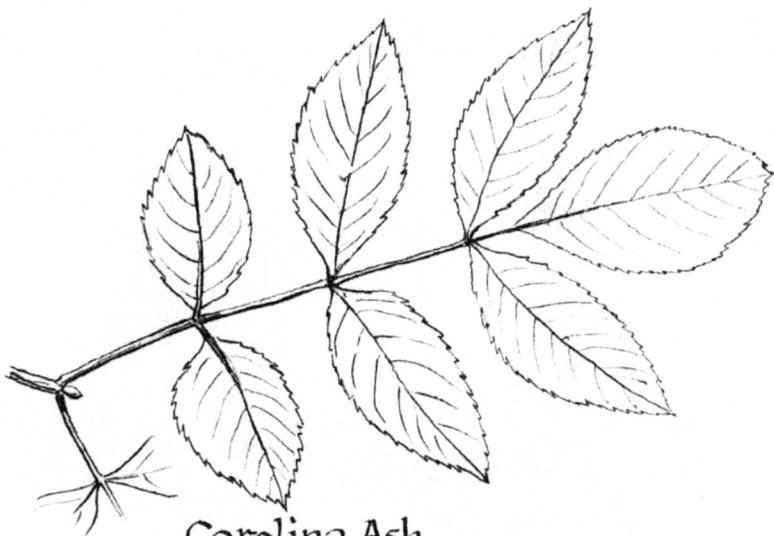

Carolina Ash
Fraxinus caroliniana

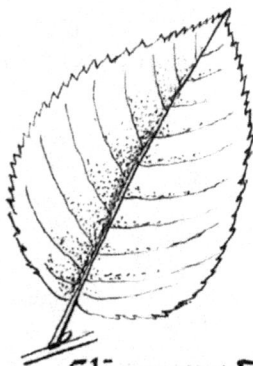

Slippery Elm
Ulmus rubra

Witch Hazel
*Hamamelis
virginiana*

Tag Alder
*Alnus
serrulata*

The ripe fruit is red.

Ogeechee
Lime or Tupelo
Nyssa ogeche

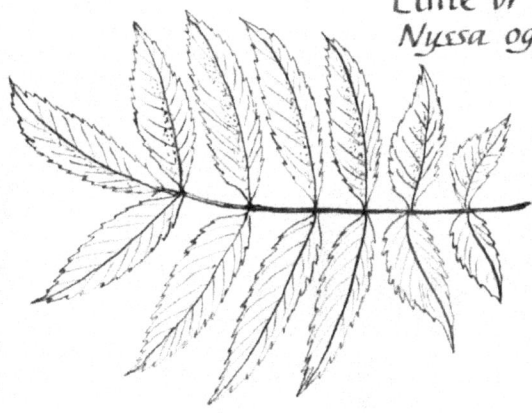

Water
Hickory
*Carya
aquatica*

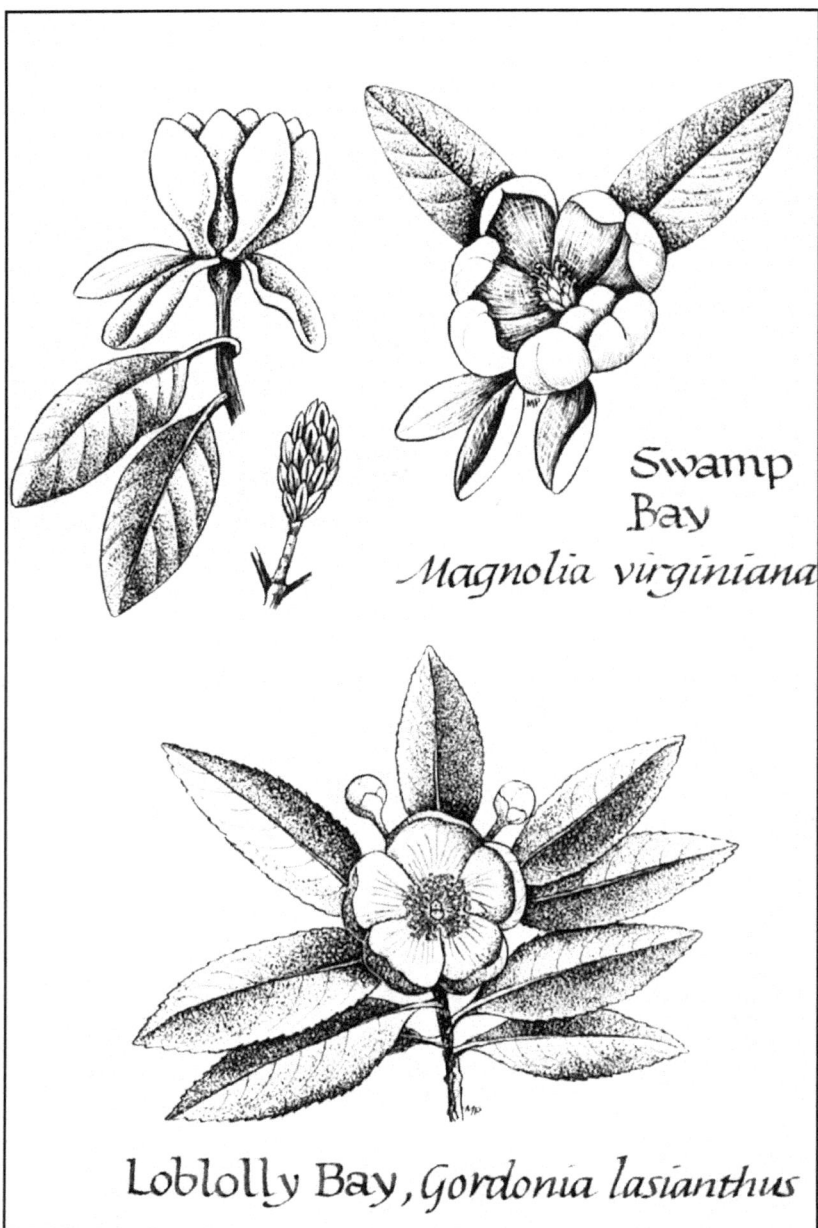

Swamp
Bay
Magnolia virginiana

Loblolly Bay, Gordonia lasianthus

Sweet
Pepper-bush
Clethra alnifolia

*graygreen leaves
are thick & leathery*

Fetterbush or
Hurrah Bush
Lyonia lucida

black berries

Gallberry
Ilex glabra

Titi
*Cyrilla
racimiflora*
*leathery
glossy
leaves*

adult

Swallow-tailed Kite

eyering

immature
Mississippi Kite

Acadian Flycatcher

Carolina Parroquet
extinct

Prothonotary Warbler

Swamp Birds

THE WETLAND BIRDS OF FLORIDA

The habitats of north Florida are similar to the habitats of Georgia, namely: coastal plain forests of pine and oak, freshwater marshes, and swamps and coastal salt marshes.The coastal salt marshes of Florida form a narrow band, unlike the vast marshes of Georgia and South Carolina. Below the midline of the Florida peninsula, the climate is tropical. The coastal salt marshes are replaced by mangrove swamps. Many tropical species of plants, including palms, flourish.

The Florida peninsula is underlain by cretaceous limestone and shale, which is dotted with sinks that often fill with water to form lakes. Florida is a land of lakes. The plants and animals of north Florida are similar to the species of the rest of the Southeast Coastal Plains.

Florida has several unique species of birds. The limpkin is a wading bird found in wetlands throughout Florida and occasionally south Georgia, as well as Central and South America. Its diet includes snails, clams, insects, frogs, lizards, and salamanders. It is a solitary bird, but occasionally it nests in loose colonies. Its nest is made of reeds and grass interwoven within a scrub, other live vegetation, or atop a stump where it lays four to eight eggs. It resembles an ibis; however, it is more closely related to rails and cranes. The limpkin is famous for its call, a wild whooping sound; its vernacular name is the "crying bird."

The limpkin is an elusive, secretive bird. In some protected refuges, it is easy to see. One of these places is the Wakulla Springs Park in the Florida panhandle. The limpkin is so accustomed to the tourist boats that traverse the channels that the boats can come close to the birds. The tall cranes are distant cousins of the limpkin.

Two species of cranes in the United States are the sandhill crane and whooping crane. The whooping crane is a spectacular bird. It stands five feet tall, the tallest bird in the United States, and is white with black wing tips and a red crown. It is a rare, endangered species.

The sandhill crane is smaller, four feet in height, gray with a red crown. The sandhill is common in many areas of the West and Midwest. The Florida sandhill crane is common from the Okefenokee Swamp through Florida. The Florida subspecies is non-migratory, but in the winter the western subspecies join the Florida crane. The Mississippi subspecies is endangered (about fifty birds remain).

Cranes are wetland birds which eat animal matter, such as minnows, small crustaceans, and insects, as well as plants, such as roots, fruit, and grain.

113

Cranes are noisy birds, making repeated trumpeting calls. The sandhill makes a harsh, almost cackling sound. but the whooping crane has a clear. clarion call, hence its name "whooping." Cranes court dramatically. Their mating rituals include bowing, leaping, and posturing movements, described as dancing. Like many birds, they are territorial during breeding, guarding their nests and surrounding area. They mate for life. The female lays two eggs; generally only one chick survives to adulthood. In winter, they are more social, feeding in groups. Sandhill cranes gather in flocks of up to a thousand, while whooping cranes form smaller flocks of nine to twelve birds.

The whooping crane was once a common and widespread bird throughout the eastern and mid-western United States. In the early 1700s, artist and naturalist Mark Catesby observed large flocks of whooping cranes at the mouth of the Savannah River during the migratory season. Since that time, the whooping crane declined. In the late 1800s, 1,500 birds existed, and by 1945, there were only seventeen. These seventeen cranes showed up every winter at the Aransas National Wildlife Refuge on the coast of Texas. At that time, nobody knew where they nested. In 1954, biologists discovered their breeding locale in the Wood Buffalo National Park in Alberta, Canada.

In an effort to increase the whooping crane population, biologists raised a captive flock, using eggs from the Canadian population. Most of the captive birds reside at the Patuxent Center in Maryland, the Calgary Zoo in Alberta, Canada, and the International Crane Foundation in Wisconsin. The captive population is now 131 birds. This captive population is the source for several programs to reintroduce whooping cranes into the wild.

In 1993, whooping crane chicks were raised in the Kissimmee Plains in Florida. The human foster parents wore "big bird" suits, and the chicks were fed by hand puppets that resembled crane heads. By these "muppet-like" methods, the young cranes grew up without becoming imprinted on human beings. These methods were so successful that now a thriving population of over forty-five whooping cranes lives in the Kissimmee Plains. These cranes have lost their migratory urge and stay in the plains throughout the year.

Another successful reintroduction program established a migratory population of whooping cranes that migrates from Wisconsin to Florida. Like many birds, young cranes learn their migration routes by following their parents. Young cranes were raised in Necedah National Wildlife Refuge in Wisconsin by human beings in crane suits. When the time came to migrate, the foster parent led the way in ultralight aircraft. The program is known as Operation Migration. The pilots began in 2001 with seven young cranes. Every year, the foster parents led young cranes to the Chassahowitzka Wildlife Refuge in Florida. The cranes return to Wisconsin on their own in the spring. Now, about sixty mature whooping cranes migrate between Wisconsin and Florida. During their travels, the cranes fly over the Carolinas and Georgia.

The recovery of the whooping crane is one of the success stories of conservation. The population grew from about seventeen in 1945 to about 500 at present, and the number keeps growing.

One other Florida bird worth attention is the roseate spoonbill. It breeds in south Florida, as well as Central and South America. In late summer, spoonbills wander and often can be seen in Georgia and the Carolinas. The adults are pink with red shoulders and a bare green head. The immature are pink with a white-feathered head. The tip of the beak is indeed shaped like a spoon!

Roseate
Spoonbill

immature

adult

Florida
Birds

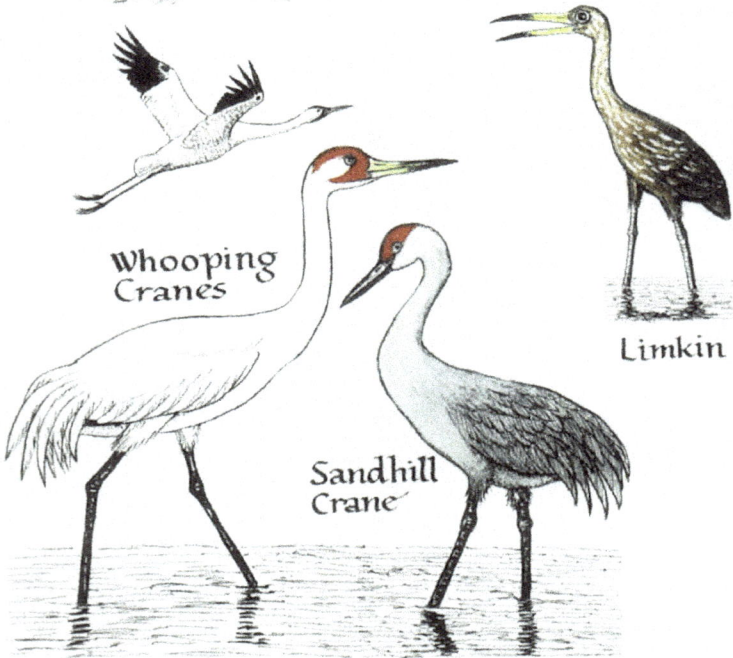

Whooping
Cranes

Sandhill
Crane

Limkin

116

III
FORESTS

COASTAL PLAIN FORESTS

Before Europeans settled the Southeast, old-growth forests covered the Coastal Plains. In the eighteenth and nineteenth centuries, much of this forest was cleared for cotton plantations, leaving little of the "virgin forest" remaining. Cotton is no longer a major crop and many acres are reverting to second-growth forests. Additionally, pine-tree farms are supplanting cotton fields as an agricultural crop. A tree farm is a monocrop, far different than a natural forest.

When William Bartram explored the forests of Georgia, Florida and the Carolinas, he encountered and described the virgin forests:

The high forests on this coast now wore a grand and sublime appearance; the earth rising gradually from the river Westward, by easy swelling ridges, behind one another, and lifted the distant groves up into the skies. The trees are of the lofty kind, as the grand Laurel Magnolia, Palma elata, Liquid-amber styraciflua [sweet gum], Fagus sylvatica [either a beech or blackgum (tupelo)], Querci [plural for oaks], Juglans hickory, Fraxinus [ash], and others.

Several types of forests grow in the Coastal Plains. These include mixed hardwoods dominated by oaks-hickories, sand hills with scrub oaks, mixed hardwood-pine forests, pine flatlands including the longleaf pine forests, wet bottomland forests often adjacent to swamps and subtropical maritime forests found on the coast.

The live oak (*Quercus virginiana*) is an evergreen oak that grows in the Coastal Plains from Virginia to east Texas and Florida. It is planted in the Piedmont region and appears to flourish there though not native to that region. It is not a tall tree, but its branches spread wide. The laurel oak (*Q. hemispherica*) is another evergreen oak often found with the live oak, These two species are widespread through the Coastal Plains, but they are the dominant trees in the Maritime Forest (discussed in Chapter 3C).

Spanish moss (*Tillandsia usneoides*) is particularly associated with live oaks. This plant is an air plant (epiphyte) that requires water vapor. The live oak exudes water vapor, so the Spanish moss flourishes on live oak branches. Spanish moss is not a parasite; it takes no nourishment from the oak. It is in the bromeliad family, which includes pineapple. It has a small yellow-green flower with three petals which ripens into an airborne seed.

Another species associated with the live oak is the resurrection fern (*Polypodium polypodioides)* that grows on the spreading oak branches. It is called "resurrection" because rain revives it. During dry spells, it is brown and dry, but after a rain, new green leaves sprout. The bracken fern (*Pteridium aguilinum*) is a common understory fern.

Several common deciduous oaks are found in the mixed oak forests of the Coastal Plains: water oak (*Quercus niger*), Southern red oak (*Q.falcata*), white oak (*Q. alba*) and black oak (*Q. velutina*). Deciduous trees shed their leaves in winter.

Water oak is semi-evergreen. In the warmer coastal regions, it drops its leaves late, but in colder areas, it is fully deciduous. In the coastal areas, the deciduous leaves only assume their bright colors in late winter, about December.

All oaks are really deciduous, but the evergreen oaks drop their leaves in the spring as new young leaves sprout. In the spring, live oaks and laurel oaks are bedecked in a delicate lacework of tiny new green leaves.

Four species of scrub oaks grow on sand hills, often among pine forests: post oak (*Quercus stellata*), turkey oak (*Q. laevis*), blackjack oak (*Q. marilandica*), and bluejack oak (*Q. incana*). These oaks are scrubby, but sometimes they reach tree size.

Oaks can be classified into two basic types: white oaks and black-red oaks. White oaks have rounded lobes and black and red oaks have pointed lobes.

The Coastal Plains have two species of common hickories: the pignut hickory (*Carya glabra*) and the mockernut hickory (*C. tomentosa*). The pecan (*C. illinoensis*) is extensively planted throughout the Southeast, but it is not native here. Its original range is the Mississippi Valley.

A tree widely dispersed throughout the Southeast is the sweet gum (*Liquidamber styraciflua*). It is a deciduous tree whose star-shaped leaves turn bright red or wine- colored in the fall. It also bears spiny spherical fruit. The evergreen *Magnolia grandiflora* is naturally restricted to the Coastal Plains ranging from South Carolina to north Florida and west to east Texas, but because of its beautiful stateliness, it is often planted elsewhere throughout the South. The magnolia is particularly common on the coast, especially in maritime forests. The tulip tree or yellow poplar (*Liriodendron tulipifera*) is a deciduous member of the magnolia family that is widespread throughout the eastern United States. Both of these magnolias have large beautiful flowers.

The black gum or black tupelo (*Nyssa sylvatica*} is widespread through the East and is frequently found in the mixed hard-

119

wood forest of the Southeast Coastal Plain. The leaves of the tupelo form clusters at the ends of the branches, and it produces dark blue-purple berries at the close of summer. Its size varies from shrub-like to a large tree.

Two members of the elm family grow in scattered locales in the Coastal Plains. The American elm (*Ulmus americanus*) is restricted to some high bluffs bordering rivers. Sugarberry or Southern hackberry (*Celtis laevigata*) grows on high ground on the coastal islands. American beech (*Fagus grandiflora*) is a common forest tree in the mountains, Piedmont and the Northeast, but it is uncommon in the Coastal Plains. Slippery elm (*Ulmus rubra*) grows in swamps.

BOTTOMLAND FOREST

The bottomland forest has a different collection of trees although the aforementioned trees may be found there. Bottomland forests grow on floodplains and the edges of rivers and swamps where the soil is wet or periodically inundated.

Willow (*Salix* spp.), sycamore (*Platanus occidentalis*), and red maple (*Acer rubrum*) are typical bottomland trees. The red maple is the only maple found in the Southeast Coastal Plain, although several species of maples are in the Piedmont and Appalachians. The leaf stems (petioles) are red, and the whole leaf turns red in the fall. Cottonwood (*Populus* spp.) is a widely dispersed bottomland tree, more common in the Carolinas than in Georgia. The river birch (*Betula niger*) is found in the Coastal Plains, but it is more prevalent in the Piedmont.

Two species of oak prefer wet soil: swamp chestnut oak (*Quercus michauxii*) and diamond leaf or swamp laurel oak (*Q. laurifolia*). The narrow-leafed willow oak (*Q. phellos*), also a bottomland oak, is more common in the Carolinas than the Georgia Coastal Plain. Many of these trees are associated with cypress swamps.

Two small trees that resemble each other are typical wet-soil trees, and both are known as bays: loblolly bay (*Gordonia lasianthus*) and sweet bay or swamp bay (*Magnolia Virginiana*).

SHRUBS & VINES

A complete, natural forest has an understory: plants that grow under the canopy, such as small trees, shrubs, vines, and ephiphytes; and ground plants, such as herbs and ferns. The Coastal Plain has a rich collection of small trees and shrubs.

The American holly (*Ilex opaca*), the "Christmas holly", can be a shrub or a tree up to seventy feet. Its range is broad, from the mountains to the maritime forests north to New Jersey and Pennsylvania, and south to north Florida. The southeastern Coastal Plain has several species of shrub hollies, of which the most abundant is yaupon holly (*Ilex vomitoria*). Gallberry (*Ilex glabra*) is common in moist soil adjacent to rivers and swamps.

Yaupon has red berries in the winter, called "Christmas berry" by locals, but its leaves are notched with tooth-like edges (crenate) rather than spiny. *Vomitoria* refers to the story that Indians made a purgative tea from its leaves. Gallberry has black berries when ripe.

Several species of blueberries are spread through the Coastal Plains. The most common are sparkleberry or tree blueberry (*Vacinium arboretum*) and highbush blueberry (*V. corymbosum*). The market variety of blueberries is a cultivar of high bush blueberry. The wild ones are smaller but equally delicious. Sparkleberries are edible and sweet, though smaller and full of tiny seeds.

Devilwood or wild olive (*Osmanthus americanus*) is another common shrub restricted to the Coastal Plains. It has olive-like berries, but other than wildlife, no one is likely to eat them.

The laurel family (*Lauraceae*) has two representatives in the southeastern Coastal Plains: sassafras (*Sassafras albidum*) and red bay (*Persea borbonia*). Both have culinary applications. Sassafras, a deciduous shrub or tree, is widespread throughout the East. The bark or roots of sassafras were used to make sassafras tea, which is the flavor in root beer. The leaves of sassafras are dried and ground to make gumbo file, an ingredient in Creole cuisine. The sassafras leaves are either oval or lobed, and a sassafras shrub has both forms of leaves.

The evergreen red bay is only found in the Coastal Plains ranging from North Carolina to eastern Louisiana and south through Florida. Commonly a shrub, it can become a tree sixty feet high, two feet in diameter. The red bay is a close relative of the European bay laurel (bay leaf), and like its relative, its leaves can be used to flavor sauces, soups, and stews. Bay leaves are subject to leaf midges and many of the leaves have galls containing midge larvae.

Other small trees found in the coastal forests include black cherry (*Prunus serotina*), laurel cherry (*Prunus carolinensis*), Chinquapin (*Castanea pumila,* a relative of the chestnut), hornbeam or ironwood (*Carpinus caroliniana*), flowering dogwood (*Cornus florida*) and red buckeye (*Aesculus pavia*). Usually these "trees" are only shrub size.

Wax-myrtle or Southern bayberry (*Myrica cerifera*) is an evergreen shrub, occasionally a tree found throughout the Coastal Plain

121

from Virginia to East Texas and Florida. Although it may grow in the forest understory, it is commonly an edge plant, especially in coastal regions, behind dunes and at the edges of salt marshes. Its aromatic leaves can be used as insect repellants.

While this chapter covers the most commonly seen shrubs and trees, other less common species grow in this region. For comprehensive coverage, see the specific botanical references listed in the bibliography.

Important components of the understory are the vines which wrap themselves around the trees and shrubs. Twenty to thirty percent of the leaf litter on the ground are vine leaves. Dense tangles of vines provide cover for wildlife, particularly small birds and their nests. Since most vines have berries, they also provide food.

The grapes are the largest vines, hanging from the trees in thick woody coils, loops, and knots, like tropical lianas. Muscadine (*Vitis rotundifolia*) and fox grape (*V. labrusca*) are the most common species. Virginia creeper (*Parthenocissus quiquefolia*) and pepper vine (*Ampelopsis arborea*) are in the grape family. They do not grow as large, but they have grape-like fruit. Grape vines are deciduous. Grape leaves turn yellow in the fall, Virginia creeper and pepper vine leaves turn red or wine-colored. Virginia creeper has compound leaves with five leaflets. If a vine is found with three leaflets, it should be left alone. It is poison ivy! However, a harmless thorny vine may have three leaflets or more, dewberry (*Rubus trivialis*). It has beautiful white flowers which become delicious blackberries. Birds or raccoons may eat them before people have a chance.

A group of evergreen thorny vines is known as briar (*Smilax* spp.). The leaves of the various species have different shapes: arrow-shaped, heart-shaped, thin and narrow. Their names are greenbrier, catbrier, sawbriar, or bamboo vine. They produce berries which provide food for wildlife. Briar will form dense entanglements around shrubs and tree trunks, and "briar-patches" in open areas at the marsh edges and the leeward side of seaside dunes.

The most beautiful vine is the trumpet vine (*Campsis radicans*), which bears lovely trumpet-shaped red flowers. It is found in scattered locations, climbing up trees.

CONIFERS

The eastern red cedar (*Juniperus viginiana*) is the most widespread of the conifers found in thirty-seven states, including the Coastal Plains of Georgia and the Carolinas. Near the coast, it is replaced by the southern red cedar, (*J. silicola*), a close relative, perhaps a subspecies. As the scientific name indicates, these trees are not cedars, but junipers. The mature cones are fleshy and berry-like. Although sometimes junipers may grow in a cluster, they are often single trees surrounded by hardwoods. The young junipers have spiny leaves; as the tree matures, the leaves become scale-like.

The Coastal Plains are noted for their pine forests. The Coastal Plains have four common species of pines: shortleaf pine (*Pinus echinata*), loblolly pine (*P. taeda*), slash pine, (*P. elliotti*) and longleaf pine (*P. palustris*). The shortleaf pine has the shortest needles (two and a half to five inches, grouped in clusters, or fascicles, of two or three), but this pine is more prevalent in the Piedmont than the Coastal Plain. The slash pine has needles seven to twelve inches long (two and three per fascicle); the loblolly needles are six to nine inches long (three per fascicle); the longleaf pine has the longest needles, ten to eighteen inches (three per fascicle).

The slash pine is more vulnerable to damage by frost than the loblolly pine. Therefore, the slash is more abundant near the coast where it is warmer, while the loblolly is the common pine inland. Pines are early succession trees. When a land becomes vacant, either by fire or clearing by humans, pines are the first to take root and grow. Young pines need full sunshine to grow. When the pines mature and shade the ground, young hardwoods, such as oaks, take root and supplant the young pines. Young hardwoods tolerate shade. In time, the forest becomes mixed hardwoods with old pines. Ultimately, the old pines die and the forest becomes a pure hardwood forest.

Pine forests depend on fire to maintain themselves. Pines can manage to survive a fire, but the hardwoods succumb to it.

Longleaf pines are adapted to fire. This is a unique ecosystem with special characteristics and wildlife. Because the wood was hard, durable, and desirable, millions of acres of longleaf pine were clear-cut for lumber. Many of these acres were replaced by loblolly pine tree farms, Nowadays, great efforts are made to preserve the remaining acres and replant the longleaf pine. The next chapter describes the longleaf pine forest in more detail.

Coastal Plain Forests

EVERGREEN OAKS

Live oak
Quercus.
virginiana

Laurel oak
Quercus
hemispherica

Water oak
Quercus niger

The live oak leaves are glossy above and "fuzzy" underneath.
The other oak leaves are smooth on both sides.

Willow
Oak
Quercus
phellos

Laurel
Oak

The bark of the Laurel Oak is "smoother" than the live oak.

Live oak

124

White Oak
Quercus alba

Black Oak
Quercus velutina

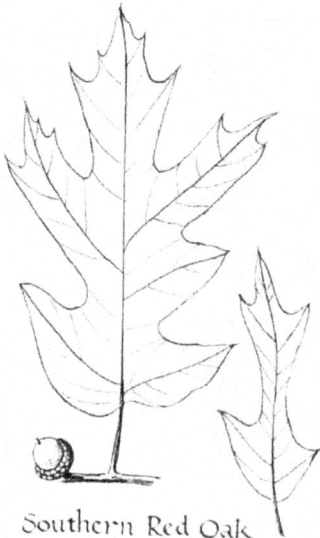

Swamp Chestnut Oak
Quercus prinus

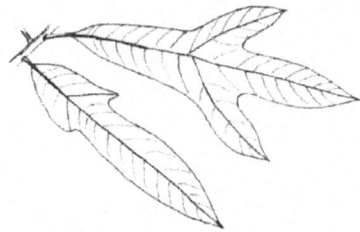

Southern Red Oak
Quercus falcata

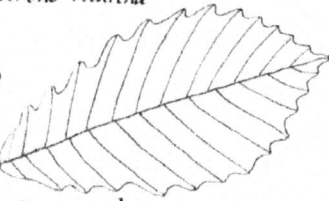

Diamond Leaf *or* Swamp Laurel Oak
Quercus laurifolia

SCRUB OAKS

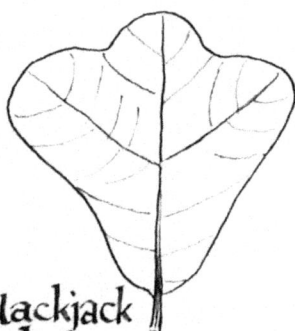

Blackjack
Oak
Quercus marilandica

Post
Oak
Quercus   stellata

Bluejack Oak
Quercus incana

Turkey Oak
Quercus laevis

Pecan
*Carya
illinoenis*

Mockernut
Hickory
Carya tomentosa

Hickory
Family

Pignut Hickory
Carya glabra

Southern Magnolia
Magnolia grandiflora

Magnolia
Family

Tuliptree
or
Yellow
        Poplar
*Liriodendron
tulipifera*

Blackgum or
Black Tupelo
Nyssa sylvatica

Red
Maple
Acer rubrum

Sycamore
Plantanus occidentalis

The bark of sycamore
is flakey revealing
white patches

Cottonwood
Populus deltoides

Willow *Salix spp.*

Bottomland Trees

Tree bark

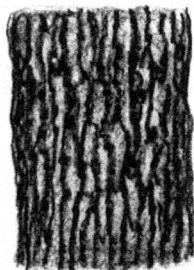

Most hardwoods
have furrowed bark

Southern
Magnolia
*Magnolia
grandiflora*

Sycamore
*Platanus
occidentalis*

peeling bark

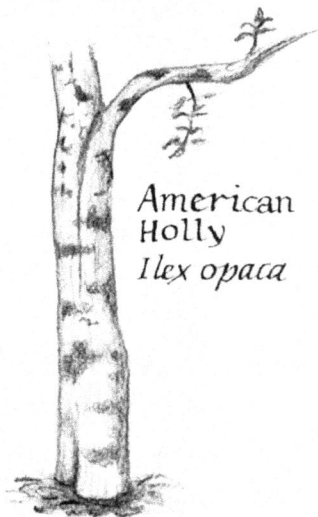

American
Holly
Ilex opaca

Sweet Gum
Liquidamber styracaflua

young needles are spiney; mature needles are scales.

Red Cedar
Juniperus virginiana

Elm
Ulmus americana

Beech
Fagus grandiflora

Sugarberry or Hackberry
Celtis laevigata

Chinquapin
Castanea pumila

River
Birch
Betula nigra

flakey bark

bark

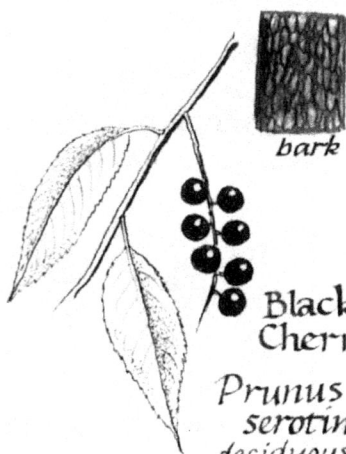

Black
Cherry
*Prunus
serotina*
deciduous

Laurel Cherry
Prunus caroliniana
evergreen

132

Sassafras
*Sassafras
albidum*

Wax-myrtle *or*
Bayberry
Myrica cerifera

Winged sumac
Rhus copallina

midge gall
Red Bay
Persea borbonia

opposite leaves

Wild Olive
or Devilwood
*Osmanthus
americana*

Yaupon Holly
Ilex vomitoria

Shrubs *or* Small Trees

133

Blueberry
Vaccinium arboretum

Dogwood
Cornus florida

zigzag twigs
Hornbeam
Carpinus caroliniana

American Holly
Ilex opaca

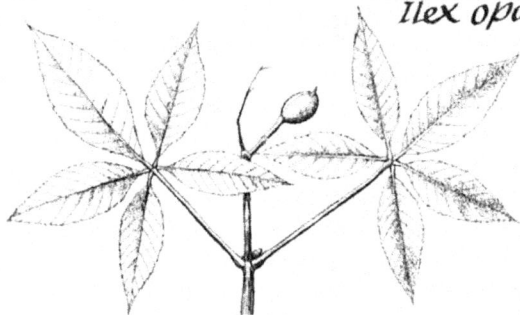

Red Buckeye, *Aesculus paira*

Vines

Virginia Creeper
Parthenocissus quinquefolia

Peppervine
Ampelopsis arborea

Muscadine Grape
Vitis rotundifolia

Grape Family

Briar
Smilax spp.

Poison Ivy
Toxicodendron radicans

Dewberry
Rubus trivialis

Passion Flower
Passiflora incarnata

flower   seed

Spanish Moss
Tillandsia usneoides

Ressurrection
Fern
Polypodium
polypodioides

grows on
oak branches

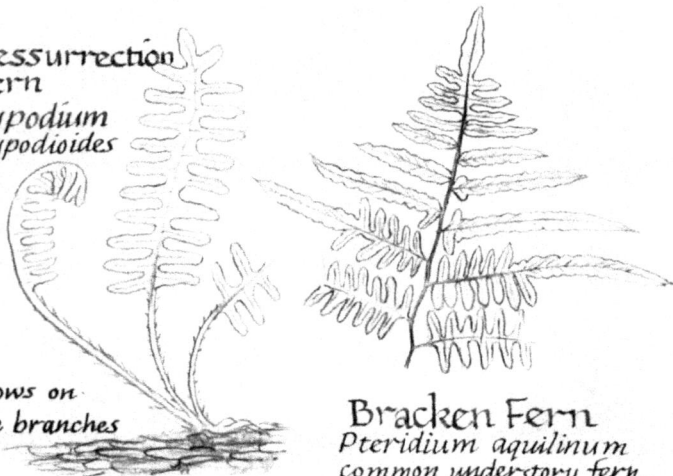

Bracken Fern
Pteridium aquilinum
common understory fern

SOUTHEASTERN PINES

Slash
Pine
2 & 3 needles
per bundle
Pinus elliotti

Loblolly
Pine
3 needles per bundle
Pinus taeda

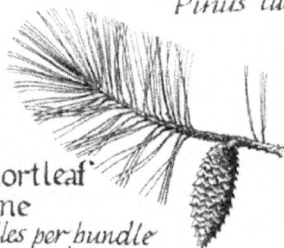

Shortleaf
Pine
2 & 3 needles per bundle
Pinus echinata

LONGLEAF PINE FOREST

The longleaf pine forest of the Southeast is a fire ecosystem. The mature longleaf pines, which can live 500 years, will survive rapidly moving ground fire.

The ground cover is primarily wiregrass (*Aristida stricta*), which readily burns when lightning strikes, creating a rapidly moving, low-intensity fire. The young pines have developed the ability to survive a fire.

If fire is suppressed, hardwoods, such as sweet gum, hickory and oak will take over and crowd out the young pines.

At one time, an estimated 85 million acres of longleaf pine forest stood in the Southeast; today, 200,000 acres, mostly second growth, remain. Of this, less than 10,000 acres of virgin old growth remain. Most of these acres are controlled by land trusts, conservancies, the military, and the Tall Timber Research Stations. These forests are managed by periodic controlled burns. The longleaf pine forests have been replaced by tree farms of fast-growing loblolly pine.

Janisse Ray in her autobiography, *Ecology of a Cracker Childhood*, lovingly describes the disappearing longleaf forests:

> Over the decades the fury and constancy of lightning knew no end - every few years it would burn the place again - and the greenhorn pines learned to lay low, sometimes for five or six years, drilling a taproot farther and farther into the moist earth, surviving the fast-burning, low-intensity fires of lightning's wrath by huddling, covering their terminal buds with a tuft of long needles. Sometimes the buds steamed and crackled inside their bonnets.
>
> Young trees that mimicked grass survived fire. That low, they didn't look like trees.
>
> The grass-trees began to learn that if they waited until the lightning went to sleep in the rainy springs and suddenly cast themselves upward, to the height of a yard or more in one season, drawing nutrient reserves from their long, patient roots, and if they hurriedly thickened the bark of their trunks, a lamination, then when the fires came again, they could withstand the heat and their terminal bud would be out of flame's reach. Only then would the trees dare to branch.
>
> Longleaf and lightning began to depend on each other and other plants—the ground cover grasses and forbs, or flowering herbs—evolved to survive and welcome fire as well. Wiregrass, for instance, would not reproduce sexually in lightning's absence. The animals learned to expect fire and to adapt. They scrambled off or took cover: down into tortoise burrows, up

into tree crowns.

During the fire, exotic insects never otherwise seen would scurry from the plates of bark, scooting up the tree. Snakes and tortoises would dash for their holes. Longleaf became known as the pine that fire built.

The longleaf pine ecosystem is open, with trees spaced far apart. The ground cover is primarily wiregrass that grows in clumps about a foot tall, all the blades growing basally from the ground. Scattered among the wiregrass are other grasses, flowering herbs, ferns, dwarf shrubs, and vines such as muscadine or *Smilax* which climb the pine trunks.

The longleaf pine (*Pinus palustris*) grows tall (100 feet) with most of the branches at the top. The bark is covered with thick, scaly, flaky, reddish-brown plates. The longleaf has the longest needles of the southeastern pines (ten to eighteen inches), three needles per fascicle (rarely two per fascicle). The mature cones can be six to ten inches long, the scales keeled with a prickle. For the first three to five years or longer, the young longleaf pine resembles a clump of grass. The bud is protected from fire by the compact arrangement of needles around the bud.

The "grass stage" blends with the wiregrass around it. When the wiregrass burns, the grass stage survives and continues to grow.

William Bartram, who explored the Southeast in 1791, called the longleaf pine ecosystem a "vast forest of the most stately pine trees that can be imagined."

Scattered through the pine forest are sandy ridges with scrub oaks: turkey oak (*Quercus laevis*), post oak (*Q. stellata*), blackjack oak (*Q. marilandica*), and bluejack oak (*Q. jacana*).

Pinus palustris means a pine living in a swamp; however, the longleaf pine grows in well-drained sandy soil. Nonetheless, the pine forest often has wet depressions among the pines. These depressions are known as pine savannahs or herb bogs and are full of plants that grow in wet soil, especially carnivorous plants like Pitcher plants (*Sarracenia* spp.) and sundews (*Drosera rotundifolia*). These plants trap insects and digest them to provide necessary nitrogen supplements.

The herb bogs are also home to a variety of colorful flowers, including orchids, lilies and composites (daisies).

LONGLEAF WILDLIFE

The longleaf pine forest is home to a variety of wildlife, including fox squirrels, pine warblers, woodpeckers, cardinals, Carolina wrens, towhees and bobwhite quail. Bobwhites live in open and brushy habitats, but much of this habitat is being destroyed by agricultural and housing developments, resulting in a decline in bobwhite populations. Bobwhites avoid deep woods, but the open grasslands of the longleaf pine forest provide perfect habitat. The towhee also likes open country of brush and grasslands.

Two species of birds prefer longleaf pine forests to any other habitat: Bachman's sparrow and the red-cockaded woodpecker.

Bachman's sparrow is a ground-dwelling bird. It forages among the ground cover, eating insects, seeds, and snails. It builds its nest on the ground, composed of grasses, herbs, and hair in a cup or dome shape, sheltered by grass, vines, or low shrubs.

Audubon describes the nest of Bachman's sparrow:

Purely by chance we came upon a female nesting in a grassy dome she had erected over a shallow depression. The nest was shielded by a clump of palmettos, and we happened upon it by watching a bird disappear, then going to that entrance. It was not yet May and three glossy white eggs cradled in her nest. Later I found nests with four and five eggs, never more, and learned that the young hatched within a matter of ten revolutions of the planet.

Bachman's Sparrow is a dull-colored bird: buff-gray and brown. It is a declining species because the open pine forests that it prefers are disappearing. It avoids the densely planted pine tree farms.

This sparrow's population was declining even during Audubon's day. The following passage is extracted from a letter that Audubon wrote to his friend, John Bachman, a Lutheran minister who lived in Charleston, South Carolina. Audubon had named this sparrow after his friend.

Only a few thousand acres of virgin old-growth longleaf pine re-main. As the old longleaf savannas are logged...your sparrows are unable to nest in the dense underbrush that springs up. The bird prefers older stands because the thick ground cover means safety—cleared forests are only briefly suitable, before woody undergrowth shades out the forbs, the broad-leaved flowering plants. The last he'd heard, the songbird was extirpated from Maryland; almost gone from Tennessee, Virginia, and Georgia; and in the serious decline in Florida, where he had recently seen them.

We can pass through the longleaf on the way to the prairie. For a second time I will be able to show you the bird who so honorably bears your name. If we are fortunate, red wolves will be calling.

Your affectionate servant,
John James Audubon

140

The red-cockaded woodpecker is well-adapted to the longleaf pine, but they may nest in loblolly or slash pines. Old-growth longleafs are subject to heartwood fungus rot, which does not kill the tree. However, the inner core of the tree is soft, enabling the red-cockaded to chisel a cavity inside the tree. Most woodpeckers make their nesting cavities inside dead trees or dead branches. The red-cockaded is one of the few woodpeckers that nest in living trees. The pine exudes sticky resin from the chiseled hole which deters nest predators, especially snakes.

The red-cockaded is not spectacular like the pileated or ivory-billed woodpecker. It is a small black and white bird with white cheeks. The cockade is a tiny red spot on the side of the head of the male, only visible when close to the bird.

The red-cockaded is a social woodpecker, forming a clan consisting of a mated pair plus the grown young, typically males, who stay with the family and help to raise the young. The clan consists of three to seven birds. These woodpeckers mate for life, and they can live up to eight years. The descendents may continue to occupy the home cavity for forty to fifty years. The defended home territory can be 100 to 200 acres. Their primary diet is wood-boring beetles that they chisel from the pine trees, but they also eat seeds and fruit. The survival of the red- cockaded woodpecker is dependent on the survival of the longleaf pine forest.

This forest is home to two endangered reptiles: the gopher tortoise and the indigo snake. The gopher tortoise lives in this forest because of the sandy soil, not because of the pines. This tortoise is a digger, and the sandy soil is easier to dig. It makes burrows that can be ten feet deep and forty feet long. The tortoise emerges from its burrow in the morning to forage for grass, leaves, and berries, and returns during the heat of the day. The size of the tortoise ranges from six inches to fifteen inches.

The box turtle is a woodland turtle common throughout the East. It resembles the gopher tortoise, but is smaller, four and a half to six inches. It is not a tortoise, but a relative of the water terrapin. It is dark with lighter splotches, which in the most common subspecies are orange.

The tortoise burrows become homes for many animals, gopher frogs, raccoons, opossums, and many species of snakes, including the diamondback rattlesnake. The burrows provide shelter for the indigo snake during cold weather. The indigo snake ranges from the Georgia Coastal Plains through Florida. In Florida, this snake is found in a variety of habitats, including mangrove swamps, but in Georgia, its primary habitat is the longleaf pine forest. It stays in this habitat because the gopher tortoise provides its winter homes.

The diamondback rattlesnake, which can grow to eight feet, is the heaviest North American snake, though the indigo snake is the longest (up to nine feet). The indigo is a beautiful snake, a shiny blue-black with an orange or red chin. It eats small mammals, birds, frogs, and snakes, including the rattlesnake. In the past, the indigo snake was popular with "snake charmers."

The longleaf pine forest is a beautiful ecosystem with unique wildlife that prefer that habitat. Because the wood of longleaf pine is strong, hard, and durable, much of that forest was harvested for timber. Most of the remaining longleaf forests are now protected and are subjected to periodic burns to protect the ecosystem. If we remain committed to protecting this ecosystem and its wildlife, then the longleaf pine forests will have a bright future.

Janisse Ray says, "We can mean that we will allow the cutover forests to return to their former grandeur and pine plantations to grow wild."

SOUTHEAST Longleaf Pine Forest

Longleaf Pine
Pinus palustris

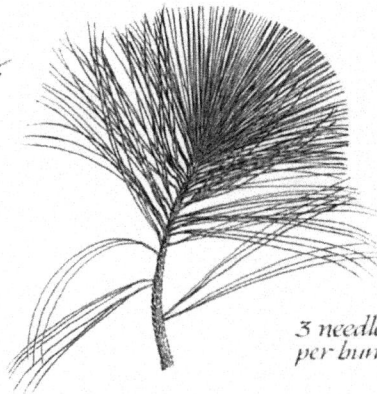

3 needles per bundle

143

Longleaf Pine Forest
understory plants

Pitcher Plants
Sarracenia spp.

Wiregrass
Aristida stricta

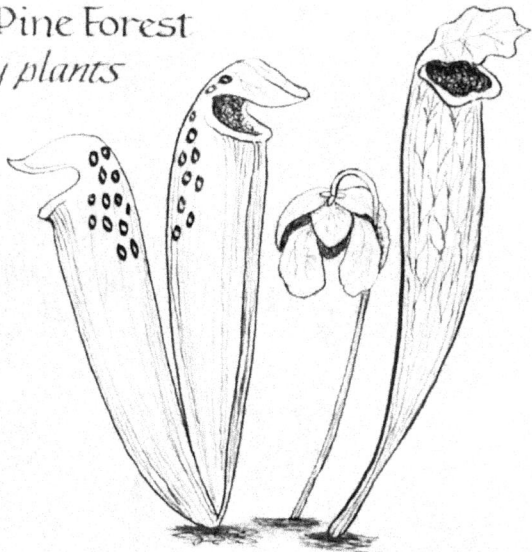

Sundew
Drosera spp.

Red-cockaded
Woodpecker

Bachman's
Sparrow

Towhee ♂
female is brown

Bobwhite

Birds of the
Longleaf
Pine Forest

Diamondback
Rattlesnake
Crotalus adamanteus

Indigo Snake
Dymarchon couperi

Gopher Tortoise
Gopherus polyphemus

Reptiles *of the*
Longleaf Pine
Forest

Box Turtle
Terrapene carolina

Amphibians & Reptiles

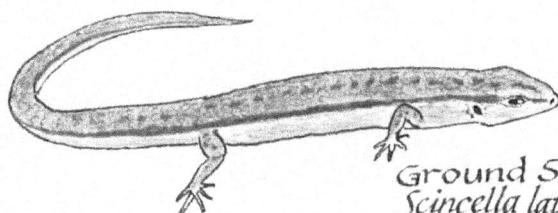

Ground Skink
Scincella lateralis

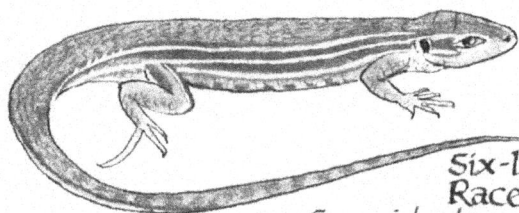

Six-lined
Racerunner
Cnemidophorus sexlineatus

Garter Snake
Thanophis sirtalis

with
flared
neck

Hognose Snake
Heterodon spp.

Copperhead
*Agkistrodon contortrix
venemous*

King Snake
Lampropeltis getula

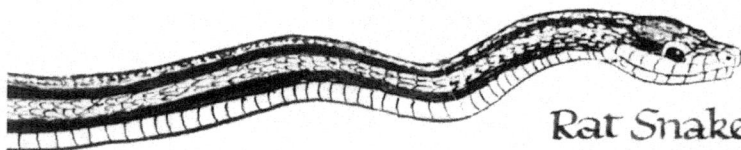

Rat Snake
Elaphe obsoleta

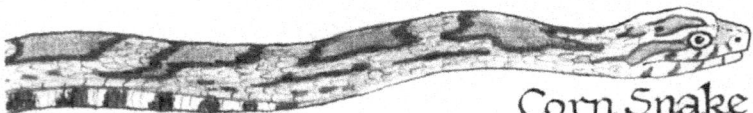

orange or russet

Corn Snake
Elaphe guttata

Black Racer
Coluber constrictor

Rough Green Snake
Opheodrys aestivus

148

cranial knobs between eyes

Southern Toad
Bufo terrestris

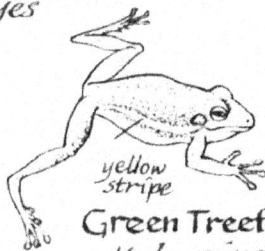

yellow stripe

Green Treefrog
Hyla cinerea

Green Anole
Anole carolinensis
green or brown

displaying male

Squirrel Treefrog
green or brown
Hyla squirella

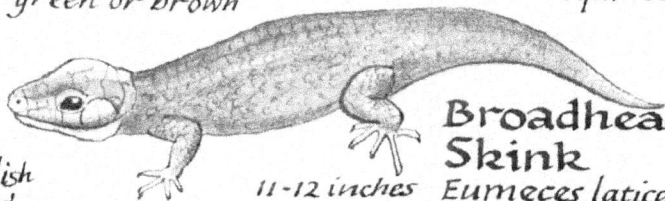

reddish head

11-12 inches

Broadhead Skink
Eumeces laticeps

Glass Lizard
Ophisaurus ventralis

MARITIME FORESTS

The name "maritime" refers to the forests by the sea on coastal islands from South Carolina to northern Florida. These coastal islands are also known as "barrier islands" because they function as barriers between the coastal storm surges and the mainland.

Because of the ameliorating effect of the sea, the coastal islands have a microclimate, a wet, subtropical climate that is a few degrees warmer than a few miles inland. The maritime forest is a subtropical evergreen forest which is a transition between the temperate forests to the north and west and the tropical forests of south Florida.

During the past 40,000 to 10,000 years of the Ice Ages, when the glaciers advanced then melted, the shore retreated, as much as 100 miles offshore, and advanced, creating and destroying a series of sand ridges which became islands, surrounded by low-lying marshes. These sand ridges, which were once ocean-facing dunes, are what we call "hammocks." The coastal islands are young, about 4,000 to 10,000 years old (the Holocene Era). The more inland islands are older.

Although the coastal islands have periodic frosts, they are less frequent and less severe than the frost a few miles inland. Two palms are typical of this "subtropical" zone: the tall cabbage palm (*Sabal palmetto*) and the dwarf sawtooth palmetto (*Serenoa repens*). The trunk of the sawtooth grows sprawling along the ground, and the stems of the leaves have sawtooth edges. Sawtooth palms form dense thickets underneath the pines and oaks of the maritime forest. The fruit of these palms are popular food for birds and raccoons. The palm berries taste like a bitter date. Raccoon feces on the coast often have palm seeds.

Still to this day, coastal islands are eroding and accreting, as sand is washed away or deposited. Newly created ridges or hammocks undergo plant succession. Dune vegetation grows first, followed by brush land. The dominant plants of the brush are wax myrtle or southern bayberry (*Myrica cerifera*), southern red cedar (*Juniperus silicola*); and cabbage palm. These plants grow behind the primary dunes or at the edges of the marsh, sometimes in dense thickets. The red cedar is actually a juniper, not a cedar, and is closely related to the eastern red cedar (*Juniperus virginiana*). In some cases, *J. silicola* grows right at the marsh, its roots covered by the high tide. Some ancient red cedars have a diameter of five feet. Red cedar and wax myrtle both have separate male and female plants (dioecious). In some cases, dense thickets of cedar or wax-myrtle may grow on the hammocks or behind the dunes.

150

Two other small deciduous trees can often be found in the transitional and edge brush land: buckthorn and prickly ash. Both species are frequently thorny. Buckthorn (*Bumelia* spp.) is a scrubby tree with berries; its leaves grow in clusters.

Prickly ash, toothache tree, or Hercules club (*Zanthoxylum clava-herculis*) is a small tree (twenty to thirty feet) restricted to the coastal regions. Its branches have thorns, and its bark is covered with protuberances that terminate with a sharp prickle. It is called the "Toothache tree" because its compound leaves contain a substance, Xantholin, similar to Novocain, that if chewed will numb a person's mouth and gums.

Pines are an early succession plant. They need full sunshine to grow. As the pines mature and shade the ground, shade-tolerant hardwoods, such as oaks, take root. As the oaks grow, the deep shade they provide inhibits the young pines, so the forest becomes an oak forest mixed with old pines, a mature climax maritime forest. The most common pine on the coastal islands is the slash pine (*Pinus ellioti*).

The climax maritime forest is dominated by two species of evergreen oaks: live oak (*Quercus virginiana*) and laurel oak (*Q. hemispherica*). The water oak (*Q. niger*) can be found in limited numbers on the coastal islands, though it is more common inland. In the spring, the laurel oak sheds its old leaves earlier than the live oak. Near the coast, the water oak is semi- evergreen, but inland, especially in the Piedmont or to the north, it is deciduous.

Southern magnolia (*Magnolia grandiflora*) and American holly (*Ilex opaca*) often are part of the maritime forest, as well as many evergreen shrubs and small trees. The live oak is the dominant tree in the maritime forest. It is not a tall tree, but it spreads wide. William Bartram describes it well.

The Live Oaks are of an astonishing magnitude, and one tree contains a prodigious quantity of timber; yet, comparatively, they are not tall, even in these forests, where growing on strong land, in company with others of great altitude (such as Fagus sylvatica [beech], Liquidambar [sweet gum], Magnolia grandiflora [Southern magnolia], and the high Palm tree) they strive while young to be upon an equality with their neighbours, and to enjoy the influence of the sun-beams, and of the pure animating air. But the others at last prevail, and their proud heads are seen at a great distance, towering far above the rest of the forest, which consists chiefly of this species of oak ....

But the latter spreads abroad his brawny arms, to a great distance. The trunk of the Live Oak is generally from twelve to eighteen feet in girth, and rises ten or twelve feet erect from the earth, some I have seen eighteen or twenty; then divides itself into three, four, or five great limbs, which continue to grow in nearly an horizontal direction, each limb forming a gentle curve, or arch, from its base to its extremity. I have stepped above fifty paces, on a straight line, from the trunk of one of these trees, to the extremity of the limbs. It is evergreen, the wood almost incorruptible, even in the open air. It bears a prodigious quantity of fruit; the acorn is small, but sweet and agreeable to the taste when roasted, and is food for almost all animals.

The wood of the live oak is extremely hard. It was once harvested to make the old sailing ships. The hull of the war battleship, the USS Constitution, launched in 1797, now berthed in the Boston Harbor, is made of live oak wood. It was nicknamed "Old Ironsides" because cannonballs bounced off its hard oak wood sides.

The live oak lives for hundreds of years. Many oaks planted in the 1700s and early 1800s are still alive and healthy.

A closely related species, the sand live oak (*Quercus geminata*) grows in the sand dunes. Usually a shrub, this oak can grow into a small tree. Oaks and other trees growing next to the sea become "wind-pruned" into a sloped incline. The "trees" near the sea are small. The height of the trees gradually rises the further away they are from the strong ocean winds. The branches bend to the west, away from the sea winds.

The understory of the maritime forest is dense and impenetrable, consisting primarily of evergreens, shrubs, and small trees. The most abundant shrub in the understory is yaupon holly (*Ilex vomitoria*) noted for its bright red berries during the winter. The red bay (*Persea borbonia*) sometimes reaches the size of a small tree. The red bay is a close relative of the European bay laurel (bayleaf), and its aromatic leaves can be used for cooking. The wild olive or devilwood (*Osmanthus americanus*) resembles the red bay, but its leaves grow opposite from each other rather than alternately on the branch like the bay (see illustration, page 133). The bay and olive both produce berries (drupes) which are food for wildlife. The maritime forest has two species of blueberries that produce edible fruit: sparkleberry or tree blueberry (*Vaccinium arboreum*) and highbush blueberry (*V- corymbasom*). The leaves of the blueberry often turn wine color in the fall.

The laurel cherry (*Prunus carolinensis*) may reach the size of a small tree. This cherry is evergreen and its leaves have spines like a holly.

Two common shrubs on the coastal islands are deciduous. The ubiquitous winged sumac (*Rhus copalina*) turns red in the fall and bears clusters of maroon berries. This shrub is common throughout the East and is primarily an edge plant. The beauty berry (*Cal-*

152

licarpus americanus) produces clusters of edible red violet berries in late summer. Some edge plants, namely, wax myrtle, juniper, and cabbage palm are also found within the maritime forest.

Like much of the coastal plain forest, the shrubs and trees of the maritime forest are covered with an entanglement of vines. These include the evergreen briar (*Smilax*) and the deciduous vines of the grape family: muscadine, Virginia creeper, and peppervine. Bracken fern (*Pteridium aquilinum*) may cover the ground. Spanish moss (*Tillandsia usenoides*) is generally associated with the live oak, but it does not grow next to the sea. It only grows on the leeward side of the coastal islands. Apparently, it cannot tolerate the salt air.

The live oak, the wax myrtle, and the red cedar can withstand the rigors of living by the sea, such as winds, salt spray, and occasional inundation of salt water. Most plants cannot. The subtropical, wetter climate and the conditions next to the sea create a unique ecosystem that we call the maritime forest. As we move away from the sea to more inland islands or the leeward side of the larger coastal islands, we see mixed forests. The typical vegetation of the maritime forest is mixed with deciduous trees like hickory, sweet gum, southern red oak, water oak, and sassafras.

The mammals and birds of the maritime forests are generally the same as found throughout the Coastal Plain, but some species of birds are more prevalent on the coastal islands. The Atlantic Flyway of migrating birds passes through the coastal islands. During fall and spring, it is an excellent locale to see numerous species of migrating birds, especially warblers. The boat-tailed grackle's range extends up the rivers and is common in freshwater marshes, but it is more abundant on the coast. The grackle is a polygamous nesting bird that forms colonies in live oaks or palms and feeds in the marsh. This interesting social bird is described in more detail in the next chapter.

The painted bunting is the most colorful bird in the United States. Although it can be found throughout the Coastal Plain, the painted bunting is most abundant on the coast in the maritime forest and brush thickets behind the dunes. This bird is a seedeater primarily (although it does eat insects) and needs the mixed habitat of grassy areas which provide grass seed for food and areas of thick brush, preferring wax myrtles that provide shelter for nesting. Population data indicate that this bunting is declining four percent per year. To protect this unique bird, we need to preserve the maritime forest and its associated brush thickets.

The coastal subtropical maritime forest is a unique ecosystem only found on the coasts of South Carolina, Georgia, and North Florida.

153

Maritime forest Little Tybee Island, Georgia
Live oak, slash pine, cabbage palm, sawtooth palmetto

154

Maritime Forest

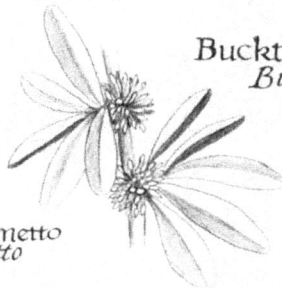

Buckthorn
Bumelia spp.

Cabbage Palmetto
Sabal palmetto

Yucca spp.

Sawtooth
Palmetto
Serenoa ripens

Spiney Ash or
Toothache Tree
*Zanoxylum
clava-hercules*

windblown oaks on dunes

Wax-myrtle
or Bayberry
Myrica cerifera

Southern Redcedar
Juniperus silicola

These plants grow at the edges of marshes
& forests and in meadows behind dunes.

Beauty Berry
Callicarpa americana

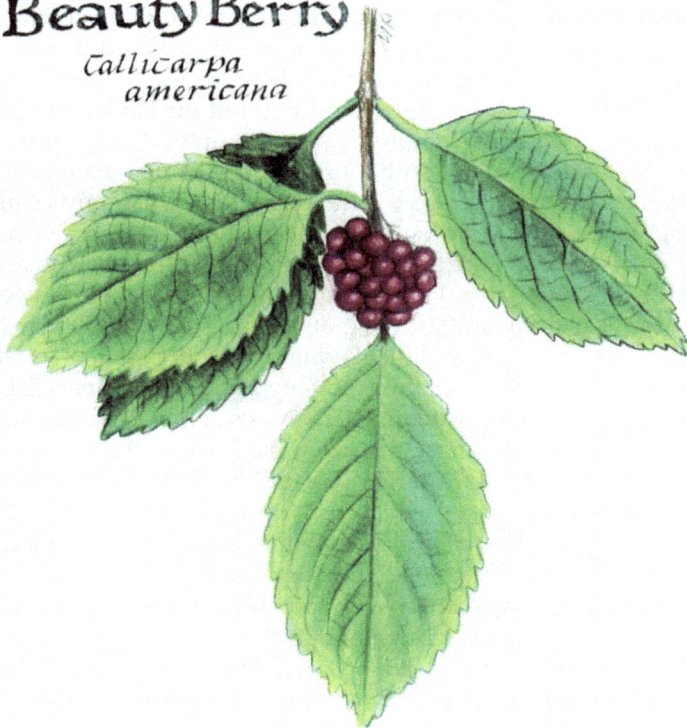

FOREST BIRDS

This section will cover the most common species of birds that inhabit the forests, including forest edges and brush areas. Most of the birds discussed are songbirds (passerine) and woodpeckers. In addition, the discussion will include night jars (nighthawk and chuck-will's widow) and the wild turkey, which Audubon called the Great American Cock. Only the most abundant and common species will be covered. The Southeastern Coastal Region is the locale of the Atlantic Flyway, so many migrants pass through this region. To identify the numerous migrants and occasionals, birdwatchers may consult one of the field guides to birds listed in the Bibliography.

The turkey is widespread throughout the United States: the East, Midwest, and portions of the West up to the Canadian border. Its range extends south into Mexico. The domestic variety descended from birds raised by the Aztecs for food. Many years ago, the population of wild turkeys had declined due to excessive hunting and habitat loss. Due to the reintroduction efforts by fish and game officials and natural propagation by the birds themselves, the populationis healthy and growing. It is a forest bird but it also likes open areas for foraging and displaying during the mating season. Its diet consists of seeds, fruit, nuts, notably acorns, some leaves, insects, and, sometimes, small vertebrates, such as salamanders or lizards. The turkey is common in the forests of the Coastal Plains, but it is only found on a few of the larger coastal islands, like Cumberland Island, Georgia.

Most people are familiar with the display postures of the male turkey, called "strutting." In many cases, a subdominant male, usually a sibling, may display with the dominant male. Occasionally, a group of males strut together. In the South, mating occurs in late January, February, and early March. The male, and sometimes the subdominant male, mates with a harem of hens, up to five or more. After mating, the hens go off by themselves to lay and incubate the eggs, which will hatch in twenty-eight days. The nest is a shallow depression in the ground lined with leaves, hidden in brush. Each hen produces ten to fifteen poults and cares for them without any help from the males. The young are precocious and run about shortly after birth. Often two or three hens may gather to raise their young together. In the winter, turkeys gather in large flocks in which a dominance hierarchy prevails (pecking order). At night, turkeys often roost in trees.

The Spaniards introduced the domesticated turkey into Europe. Europeans confused the turkey with the guinea fowl, an

African bird, which was believed to come from Turkey, hence the name of our chicken-like bird.

Woodpeckers are typically forest birds. They nest in dead trees or branches in cavities that they excavate themselves, but they may nest in bird boxes. A usual clutch is four to five eggs. We think of woodpeckers racheting up trees, bracing themselves on their stiff tail feathers, hammering into bark to seek out insects which they extract with their long barbed tongues. They also eat seeds, nuts, fruit, and sap. They may feed on the ground, especially the flicker. The loudest hammering occurs not while they are chiseling into wood for food but during mating. The male woodpecker is advertising for a mate which is why they often hammer on metal. It makes a louder sound.

The small downy woodpecker is the most widely dispersed woodpecker found in a variety of habitats from deep woods to orchards and gardens. Most woodpeckers make a deep, echoing-pulsing sound, but the downy makes a high-pitched "whinny."

The red-headed woodpecker is common throughout the forests of the Coastal Plains, though it is rare on the coastal barrier islands. This woodpecker prefers open park-like forests. Probably the dense jungle-like maritime forests are not suitable habitat for this bird. Its unisex garb is spectacular: black and white garb with an all-red head.

The red-bellied woodpecker is common in all the forests, including the maritime forests. The "red belly" is a barely discernable pink flush. The male wears a red cap, while the female only has red on the nape of the neck.

The flicker nests in trees, but it likes open areas because it is a ground feeder, preferring ants. Its underwings are bright yellow. The yellow-bellied sapsucker is a wintering bird in the southeastern coastal forests. As its name indicates, it does eat sap as well as insects and fruit.

The most spectacular woodpecker is the large (sixteen inches) pileated woodpecker with a red crest. Walter Lantz based his cartoon character "Woody Woodpecker" on this bird. Although not as common as the other woodpecker species, it is widely dispersed in mature forests, cypress swamps, even suburbs if they have trees, especially dead trees, for nesting. Its pulsing, throbbing call is haunting as it echoes through the woods.

The red-cockaded woodpecker is an endangered species whose preferred habitat is the longleaf pine forest (see Chapter 3, Section B, "Longleaf Pine Forests" for more about this habitat and its inhabitants, including the red-cockaded woodpecker).

159

Nightjars (whip-por-wills and chuck-will's widows) are typical forest birds, however, the chuck-will's widow is the one that commonly nests in the Coastal Plain. Whips nest in the Coastal Plain in small numbers. While the whip-por-will winters in the Coastal Plain, it is silent and rarely seen. Both species are nocturnal. The two species are virtually identical, but the chuck-will's widow is larger (twelve inches as opposed to the whip-por-will's ten inches), and their songs are different. The two species nest in the Piedmont. Their songs echo in the Piedmont forests. The birds' names are onomato- poeic descriptions of their songs. The southern bird's song begins with an irruptive "chuck," then proceeds to the whistled part, "will's widow." The song is a glissando, that is, the notes slide from one to another. In the whip-por-will's song, the last note is higher in pitch and extended (in musical terms, a frumata). Someone standing close to the whip-por-will will hear a preliminary "chuck" or "quirt" (see llustration for diagrams of the songs).

Nightjars feed on the wing, swallowing flying insects with their wide mouths. The larger chuck-will's widow sometimes swallows small flying birds whole. They rest on the ground or low branch, resembling a gargoyle with large eyes, froglike mouth, and small feet hidden under their puffed-out bodies. Nighjars lay their eggs, usually two, in a slight depression in the ground, not a built nest. The incubating adult, most often a female, depends on camou- flage to conceal herself. Her mottled plumage blends perfectly with the leaf litter on the ground. If disturbed, she may move her eggs to a new site. They carry the eggs either in their mouth or between the feet. They do regularly roll them using their bill.

The other common nightjar in the Southeast, and most of the Eastern United States, is the nighthawk. Not a forest bird, it prefers open areas, including grassy areas, interdune meadows,and open forests like the longleaf pine, but it may be found in cities because it nests on flat gravely roofs. Like its relatives, the nighthawk catches insects on the wing. It is active both day and night, flying high above trees on buildings, uttering a buzzing call note. It dives from a great height, then at dive's end, it brings its wings down quickly to begin its ascent, creating a distinctive "whish" sound. The nighthawk resembles other nightjars. However, the nighthawk is slender with longer wings, which has a white half-moon shape on the primary wing feathers. The nighthawk will display the "broken wing" ruse to lead predators away from its nest.

The tits are a family of small birds that reside in forests through- out the world. The two tits that live in the Southeast are the

Carolina chickadee and the tufted titmouse. These birds are permanent residents; they don't migrate. Black-capped chickadees live in northern parts of the Southeast in the Appalachian Mountains of Tennessee, Kentucky, North Carolina, West Virginia, and Virginia.

The name "titmouse" is from Anglo-Saxon, "mase" means small bird. "Tit" (originally "tittr") means something small. The name "chickadee" is an onomatopoeic word for their common call note. The black-capped chickadee is a northern species that extends into the Appalachian Mountains. In the rest of the Southeast, the black-capped is replaced by the Carolina chickadee. The two birds are almost identical; the black-capped is a little larger with stronger contrasts between the black and white on the wings. Their songs differ. The black- capped is a two-note song, "Fee-bee." The first note is higher than the second note. The Carolina has a three or four note, "fee-bee, fee-bee." The last two notes are lower in pitch than the first two notes. The two species can sometimes interbreed (hybridize) where the ranges meet.

Songs of most songbirds are learned, so regional variations exist of chickadee songs. However, the chickadee has a repertoire of calls with different meanings that is instinctual (inherited). S. T. Smith's 1972 study indicated that the Carolina chickadee has twenty different calls. In addition to the song, the calls fit into the following categories: "chickadee," gargles, twitters, hisses, tseets, dees, zees, and screams, with variations in each category. Most of the calls have social meanings, such as mating, dominance, aggression, social gathering, parental calls, begging, and warning calls (variations on the "chickadee" call) about predators.

Chickadees are social birds. In the summer, the group is a monogamous family group of the parent pair and the young. The average clutch of eggs is six. Some studies have indicated that the female may have a sexual liaison with a neighboring male, but the family group remains intact. In the winter, several chickadee families may gather together as well as with other species: titmice, nuthatches, and warblers.

Chickadees nest in tree cavities, but they will use ready-made cavities, such as bird boxes. I have observed them nesting in a remnant of an old clothesline stand, which was a tall metal tube, the end of which was bent over at a right angle. The end was an open round hole and the parents went in and out of it all day. bending in through the hole, tail at an angle, feeding their young.

The chickadee diet is onmivorous: insects, suet, fruit, and

seeds. They will climb vertically up the trunks of trees, gleaning the bark for insects and will hang upside down on small branches searching for insects. At bird feeders, their favorite food is sunflower seeds, which they carry to branches, hold in their feet, and hammer open. Their beaks are short but stout and obviously strong. Chickadees may become tame and learn to feed on an outstretched hand full of sunflower seeds.

The tufted titmouse is larger than the chickadee but its behavior is quite similar. It is also a cavity nester, and its diet is much like the chickadee, including a preference for sunflower seeds. At the bird feeder, the chickadee usually defers to the larger titmouse. The titmouse's song is a slurred "peter," the first note higher in pitch than the second. It has a large repertoire of about twenty call notes, including a "chickadee-like" call. Like the chickadee, the titmouse may become tame. Its range is widespread, throughout eastern United States up to the canadian border.

Nuthatches have unique habits. They are primarily insect-eaters, gleaning their prey from bark. They move vertically up and down tree trunks, either head-up or head-down, moving from tree to tree. In the winter, nuthatches eat seeds and fruit. They are cavity nesters with an average clutch of five. The white-breasted nuthatch is the most common nuthatch throughout the United States, including the Appalachian Mountains and the Piedmont. In the Coastal Plain, they occur in mature, open pine forests, such as the Red Hills and at Fort Stewart and Fort Benning, Georgia, but in the southeastern Coastal Plains, especially Georgia and north Florida, the brown-headed nuthatch is the most common.

The Carolina wren is common and is a permanent resident in the southeastern Coastal Plains. It likes open woods, though it is equally at home in a suburban garden with trees. Its nests are built in cavities in trees or anything else, including hanging flowerpots, any type of covered ledge, or holes in storage containers. Its song is loud and flute-like, a descending sequence of two or three notes. The singing bird is perched high, often with its tail at an angle. Sometimes, the females sing. Their call notes include a scolding "chi-chi-chi" and a trill that sounds like a telephone ring.

The monogamous pair of Carolina wrens establishes a territory where they raise their young, usually five chicks to a pair. The Carolina wren is unique in that it will sing throughout the year. As is true of most songbirds, the songs are a way of establishing their territory. The house wren and winter wren winter in the Southeast, but they are elusive and hard to see, whereas the Carolina wren boldly sings in plain view. This wren's primary diet is insects, and they will eat berries and small seeds.

The blue-gray gnatcatcher is a tiny energetic sprite whose nasal high-pitched call is heard throughout the Southeast. It is a summer resident, wintering in the Caribbean islands and Central America. The gnatcatcher lives in a variety of forests, but it loves oaks, where it often builds its nest. It is found along the forest edge or near openings or in more open forests. The nest is built of plant down, spider silk, and lichen saddled on a horizontal limb or in a fork where it is hard to see. The monogamous pair takes turns incubating the eggs (four to five) and raising the young. Gnatcatchers are primarily insectivorous, gleaning foliage for insects or spiders, often hovering and catching insects on the wing. They are active birds regularly flicking their long tails, displaying their white outer tail feathers.

The ruby-crowned kinglet is in the same family as the gnatcatcher. On the Southeast Coast, it is a winter resident. The kinglet is insectivorous, though in the winter it eats berries, including the waxy bayberry (wax myrtle, *Myrica cerifera*). This bird is small (four and one quarter inches) and gray with a white eye-ring and a white bar on the wing. The ruby crown is rarely seen, only when the male raises his crest in display. The golden-crowned kinglet also winters on the Southeast Coast, yet it stays in the crowns of tall trees, such as pines, and is hard to see. However, the ruby-crowned kinglet will feed in bushes with berries, and can be seen at eyelevel.

Kinglets and gnatcatchers are in the family *Silviidae* which, in Europe and England, are known as warblers. What we call warblers in America is in the family *Parulidae* sometimes called the wood warblers. Wood warblers are restricted to the Americas: North, Central, and South America. The old-world warblers wear drab plumage, but the wood warblers often have bright-colored plumage of yellow, blue gray, and sometimes orange.

Many species of warblers pass through the southeastern coastal regions during migration but only a handful of species reside here for long periods either in summer or winter.

The three species that reside and breed in Southeast forests during the summer are pine warbler, yellow-throated warbler, and parula warbler. The pine warbler prefers pine forests and only nests in the branches of pine trees. Like all warblers, its primary diet is insects and spiders, though it will eat berries and seeds, including pine seeds. In pine forests during the summer, the monotone trill of the pine warbler is a common sound. It has a pale yellow breast, but it is a rather drab bird with white wing bars.

163

By contrast, the yellow-throated warbler is striking, with bright yellow throat, black mask and side-streaks, and a blue-gray back with white wing bars. This warbler loves oak-pine woods and cypress swamps, often building its nest in Spanish moss. It has a beautiful song, a sequence of descending whistled notes ending with one or two rising notes.

The parula warbler is among the smallest warblers. It has a blue-gray back and yellow breast, and wears, as a cravat, a dark band bordered by orange. It lives in the canopy of mature forests where it will vigorously sing its song, a rising buzzy trill. The parula warbler builds its nest in hanging lichen or Spanish moss. Its original range in the Southeast was coastal forests, swamps, and riparian woodlands, but it has extended its range into the Piedmont and even the mountains.

The most abundant wintering warbler in the southeast coastal regions is the yellow-rumped warbler. They breed in Canada and northern United States, but they winter from Virginia and Kentucky south. In the summer, most warbler pairs form a mating territory to raise their young. In the winter, yellow-rumps, colloquially called "butter butts," form social flocks moving rapidly through the canopies or shrubbery, looking for food, constantly uttering their "tchip" call note. In the spring, after they've molted into their summer plumage, the males display aggressive behavior toward each other.

All warblers are basically insectivorous birds, but in the winter, many species will also eat berries. Yellow-rumps in particular have a decided fancy for the waxy berries of the wax myrtle. They will swarm in these bushes, eating berries. The waxy coating provides good nutrition. Other insectivorous birds, such as kinglets and swallows, eat wax-myrtle berries, otherwise known as bayberries. Because of their dietary habits, the yellow-rumped warbler is also known as the myrtle warbler. In the spring and summer, yellow-rumps wear striking garb: blue-gray and black with yellow on the side and the rump. In the winter, the plumage is more subdued, but the yellow rump always stands out as an indicator of the species.

Another common wintering warbler is the palm warbler, however, it is not a forest bird. It is an "edge" bird, residing in forest edges, brush, and the edges of marshes and dunes. The palm warbler is a plain drab bird, though its tail, which it frequently flicks, has a yellow patch under it.

The prothonotary warbler is a spectacular bird, yellow-orange head and chest and gray body. Its preferred habitat is cypress swamps or other wooded swamps. It nests in hollow trees or bird boxes throughout the Southeast.

164

The yellowthroat male has a black mask and yellow throat; the female is missing the mask. Its preferred habitat is marshes where it builds its nest in edge shrubbery or brushy fields where it usually inhabits damp areas.

Many warblers pass through the Southeast coastal region during migration. Of these, one species demands mention because it is so spectacular: the redstart. The male is orange and black. It actively pursues insects on the wing, spreading its black and orange tail. The females and young males have similar patterns, but the orange is replaced by yellow and the black is replaced by green and gray.

While the vireos resemble warblers, they are in a separate family (*Vireonidae*). Like the warblers, they are primarily insectivorous, although they will eat berries in winter. Unlike the often-colorful warblers, vireos wear plain, drab attire. The two most common vireos in the Southeast, particularly in the summer, are the red-eyed vireo and the white-eyed vireo. In addition to its red eye, the red-eyed vireo has a thin white eye-strip bordered by black above its eye. The white-eyed vireo has yellow "spectacles" around its white eye. Both species are hard to see, hidden by foliage in the canopy or shrubbery, but their songs are distinctive. The redeye sings a series of short robin-like warbling phrases. The phrases are repeated all day, often forty times a minute. The white-eye has a harsh, almost explosive song, described as *"chic"-a pureer-"chic."*

Seed-eating birds are distinguished by having stout, conical-shaped bills suitable for opening seeds, but seed eaters also eat fruit and insects.

Seedeaters superficially resemble each other, yet they are classified into several different families. Such birds are cardinals, buntings, finches, and sparrows. These birds come to birdfeeders.

Most people are familiar with the cardinal, commonly called the redbird. The male is bright red with a black mask and a crest. The female is also crested, but her plumage is overall brown with splashes of red. Young cardinals are brown with dark bills. The song of the male is a clear, beautiful whistle. Sometimes, the females sing. Cardinals are non-migratory, permanent residents. Their range is widespread, throughout eastern United States to the Canadian border and south into Mexico. The preferred habitats are brushy thickets within woods or at its edges, thickets behind dunes, and suburban gardens and parks. In the summer, the pair forms a nesting territory, raising about four young. In the winter, cardinals may gather in flocks. During courtship, the male feeds the female. A pair may raise two broods during the summer.

Two local species of related birds are known as buntings: the painted bunting and the indigo bunting. The indigo bunting is the only all-blue bird in the Southeast. The bluebird has an orange breast. The larger blue grosbeak, only occasionally observed, has brown on its wings. The painted bunting is the most colorful bird in the United States. The male has a blue head, red breast and rump, and a patch of yellow-green (chartreuse) on its back. The female painted bunting is yellow and green, the only finch-type bird with those colors. The female indigo bunting is brown.

The range of the painted bunting is restricted to the Southeast Coastal Plain from the Carolinas through the Florida peninsula. Its range is from the southern coast of North Carolina to the northeast Atlantic coast of Florida with extension inland in southwest South Carolina and southeast Georgia. It is a summer resident, wintering in the tip of Florida, the Caribbean Islands, Mexico, and Central America. A second population is found in Texas, Oklahoma, Arkansas, and Louisiana. Some ornithologists believe that this other population may be a separate species.

The indigo bunting is widely dispersed throughout the eastern United States up to the Canadian border. The indigo bunting does not live in the deep woods; it prefers forest edges, brushlands and suburban gardens and parks. Fairly common in the coastal plains, it avoids the maritime district except while it migrates.

In the forests and brushland adjacent to the ocean, the indigo bunting is replaced by the painted bunting. The painted bunting's preferred habitats are behind the dunes, brushlands, and maritime forests with plenty of shrubbery. This bunting is fond of dense thickets of wax myrtle (*Myrica cerifera*) which provide shelter for nesting. It also nests in Spanish moss. Though the painted bunting can be found at scattered sites in the Coastal Plains, it is most abundant at the coast. Since it is a seedeater, it likes adjacent grassy areas that provide grass-seed for food. It will eat dune panic grass (*Panicum amarum*) but avoids the larger seeds of the sea oats (*Uniola paniculata*). In birdfeeders, the painted buntings prefer the small millet seed and avoid the larger seed. This bird will eat insects.

The brightly colored male painted bunting is shyer than the dull-colored female. The male can be aggressive with other males. They fight with wings aflutter, butting their red breasts together. The males sing a variable melodic warble from the highest perch they can find. Sometimes immature males, resembling females, will sing.

According to collected population data, painted buntings are declining by four percent per year. Why this is happening is unclear but development is the likely culprit. The coastal area is popular and

166

every year more prime bunting habitat, especially native shrubbery, is being converted to housing developments. If developers would leave green belts of trees and native shrubbery between the houses, painted buntings and people could probably coexist in peace.

The house finch is often the most abundant bird at bird feeders. The female is mottled brown; the male has a bright magenta-red head. Originally an inhabitant of western United States, it was introduced into Long Island in the 1940s and now it is widespread throughout the East. Its primary habitats are open woods, farms and urban areas. It nests in building ledges with overhangs, hanging flower pots, vine tangles, such as ivy on buildings, and conifers. The main requirement for a nest site is an overhanging structure. It competes with the house sparrow (or English sparrow) for nesting sites.

The English sparrow was introduced in New York in 1850 and 1867. It is abundant in urban and agricultural areas and avoids deep woods. Both species are non-migratory residents.

The goldfinch is a winter visitor in the southeastern coastal plains. Its preferred habitats are weedy fields, open woodlands, forest edges, as well as gardens and urban parks. At birdfeeders, it prefers small seeds, especially thistle seed. The goldfinch is a plucky bird. It stands its ground at the feeder against larger birds, such as cardinals. In the winter, the plumage of the goldfinch is a dusky yellow, with black wings. By late spring, the male is bright yellow and black. The male's new, bright attire is a result of wear. The tips of the winter feathers are worn off, revealing bright yellow that was hidden. The male molts into new dull plumage in the fall, just before it migrates.

The white-throated sparrow, which breeds in Canada and the northeast United States, is a common winter resident in the Southeast. It is an inhabitant of woods with brushy understory, forest edges, and parks and urban gardens. Although it regularly visits birdfeeders, it commonly feeds on the ground. In its breeding range, it nests on the ground. In the summer, this sparrow establishes breeding territories, while in the winter they form flocks of five to fifteen.

The chipping sparrow is common and widespread, but in the southern Coastal Plains of Georgia and Florida, it is primarily a wintering bird. Its habitats are open woodlands, forest edges, and suburban gardens and parks. The field sparrow is resident in the Southeast throughout the year, though in Florida, it is a winter resident. As its name indicates, the habitat of the field sparrow is weedy fields and brush. These two sparrows resemble each other with

167

chestnut crowns. The chipping sparrow differs with a white stripe through the eye and a duller crown in the winter.

Several species of sparrows that are marsh inhabitants are dealt with in the marsh chapters.

Cedar waxwings show up in the Southeast during winter and in the migratory seasons. Although waxwings do eat insects, their primary diet is fruit. In the winter and migratory seasons, they move around in large flocks, seeking trees or shrubs, such as holly (*Ilex opaca* or *Ilex vomitoria*) that have ripe berries. Waxwings have been reported as getting drunk on fermented overripe fruit. As the flock moves, the birds make high-pitched "tseet" sounds, almost a lisping.

Thrushes are a worldwide family, commonly residing in forests. The most well-known thrush in the United States and Canada is the robin. Everybody is familiar with a robin "bob, bob, bobbing" along lawns, looking for and pulling up worms. Robins also eat insects and fruit. Its habitat ranges from woods to lawns and parks with trees. It breeds in the mountains and Piedmont of the Southeast. In the coastal region, a few cases of breeding pairs occur, but most robins are winter residents. While breeding, robins establish territories, yet robins form social flocks in the winter. In the coastal plains during winter, robins gather in moist woods adjacent to swamps or marshes, probably because it is easier to obtain worms and other invertebrate prey from moist soil.

The other common wintering thrush is the hermit thrush, which prefers forests with a brushy understory. It is a solitary bird, normally found alone, unlike the more social robins. The wood thrush is a summer resident, larger than the hermit thrush. It has a russet back and more spots on its chest than the hermit. The hermit is gray brown with a russet tail. The wood thrush's song is a three to five-note, flute-like phrase, ending with a trill which echoes through the otherwise quiet woods. The wood thrush prefers open hardwood forest. They need a large territory. Some ornithologists have estimated that they may need as much as forty acres. A discontinuous habitat, such as forest patches separated by open fields or lawns, seems disadvantageous to the species, possibly because it opens them up to predation or cowbird parasitism. Overall, the population of wood thrushes is declining by one to two percent per year. The wood thrush is found in scattered locales throughout the coastal plants forests and only on a few of the larger barrier islands. During migration, it does show up on the barrier islands.

The bluebird, with its blue back and orange breast, is also a thrush. They like open habitat with scattered trees. Their diet is

168

insects and berries. Originally, they lived on forest edges, nesting in found cavities, or woodpecker holes, in trees, adapting to cavities in fence posts as agriculture had expanded. As wood fences and decaying trees declined, so did the bluebird. Nowadays, bluebirds reside wherever people install bird boxes in open habitats for them to nest.

Several other species of thrush pass through this area during migration. Check one of the standard bird field guides to identify them.

Now we come to the family known as mimic thrushes: mockingbirds, brown thrashers, and catbirds. While they are not thrushes, they are called "mimics" because they mimic the songs and calls of other birds, sometimes as many as 1,000 individual phrases. Mockingbirds repeat each phrase three times or more, thrashers two times, and cat birds once. These are averages of the repeats, though variations occur. In the Southeast, mocking birds and brown thrashers are permanent residents that migrate south from the northern parts of their ranges. Catbirds have scattered breeding sites in the Southeast Coastal Plains but more catbirds are present in winter.

Mimic thrushes are territorial birds; the songs are mating calls and an announcement of their territorial claims. Mockingbirds will do a boundary dance in which they hop back and forth, facing each other with tail raised, opening and closing their wings to reveal the white patches on their wings. In the summer, they are protecting breeding territory; in the winter, the food supply. In the southeastern subtropical zone, their territory remains the same through the year. Mockingbirds are defensive during the mating season, chasing away other mockingbirds, birds that threaten their young, such as blue jays, grackles, or hawks, and even cats and human beings. Mockingbirds may swoop down just over a person's head. In the spring, mockingbirds sing constantly, even through the night. In midsummer, they are silent, with a brief spurt of singing in early fall. By late fall and early winter, they are usually quiet.

Brown thrashers' behavior is similar to the mockingbird and their song fests are just as beautiful. Thrashers customarily feed on the ground, "thrashing" about among the leaf litter, looking for insect prey. Both species eat insects, fruit, and scrap food, such as dry cat food or dog food left outdoors. Both will raise two broods a year, an average of four young per brood, building their nests in low shrubs.

While the mockingbird's original habitat was forest edges, they do quite well in suburban gardens and parks. The brown thrasher is an "edge bird," but they favor bushy woods with open areas. The brown thrasher is shyer and more elusive than the mock-

169

ingbird.

One family is known as flycatchers. And that's what they do. They wait on a tree branch until a flying insect comes by. Then they follow the insect with a zigzag flight until they catch it. Flycatchers will eat berries if insects are unavailable. The two flycatcher species common in the coastal area are the Eastern kingbird and the great crested flycatcher. Although the kingbird perches and builds its nest in tall trees such as pines, it prefers open areas. It is called "king" because it aggressively protects its territory, chasing away threats: jays, crows, hawks, cats, and sometimes human beings, dive-bombing their heads. It has a small red patch on its dark crown, which it can erect during displays.

The great crested flycatcher prefers wooded areas. It builds its nest in found cavities, woodpecker holes, or bird boxes. It makes its nest of leaves, fur, feather, and snakeskin. It raises about five young, and they migrate south as a family group. The kingbird and great crested flycatcher are summer residents, migrating to Central and South America for the winter.

Two other small flycatchers reside in the coastal plains but not in the coastal maritime forests. The Acadian flycatcher lives in riparian woodlands and cypress swamps. The wood pewee lives in hardwood forests, mixed pine hardwood forests, and open pine furests. Both are small greenish-gray birds with white wing bars, but the Acadian is distinguished by white eye-rings. They are summer residents.

The crow family, along with parrots, are considered the most intelligent of birds. In the Southeast, this family has three species: blue jays, American crows, and fish crows. A few ravens live in the Appalachian Mountains, but this large crow is more abundant in Canada, Western United States, and Eurasia. Most corvids form nesting territories in spring and early summer, while for the rest of the year they form social flocks.

The blue jay is widely dispersed, every place from deep woods to suburban gardens and parks. It has a wide range, eastern and mid-western United States to the Rocky Mountain foothills into Canada. Most people are familiar with the raucous 'jay" call, but they make other sounds, including a two-note, bell-like sound and a rattle, and soft "kueu." Their most curious call is a "squeaky hinge" sound, accompanied by a bowing motion; it is a mating call.

The blue jays form a mating territory and raise about four or five young which stay with the parents through the fall. They build lined-stick nests high up in trees. They chase away other jays, and are aggressive against predators, such as squirrels, cats, and hawks.

170

In the winter, several jay families may form social flocks.

The blue jay's diet is omnivorous and diverse: insects, seeds, nuts, fruit, nestling birds, and eggs of other birds. Their diet can include cat food and human junk food, such as potato chips and hamburger leftovers.

Crows live in a variety of habitats, ranging from woods, open areas and farms to urban areas. They are one of the most adaptable of our birds. Like the jays, their diet is omnivorous and diverse and they will raid birds' nests and scavenge leftover human food. They form nesting territories, yet other crows can associate with the nesting pair, probably young from the prior year. After the young are raised, crows form large social flocks that gather at designated roosting sites every night. Everybody knows the standard "caw," but crows have a range of calls, which probably are related to socialization. When male crows mate, they make a "coo" sound to the female, accompanied by bowing with spread wings.

In the Southeast coastal region, a smaller crow is known as the fish crow. When fish crows feed with common crows, the size difference is obvious. The two species make different sounds. The fish crow makes a nasal "haw" sound and a negative "ugh ugh!" Some people call this crow the "ugh ugh" bird!

Common crows and fish crows do not hybridize. Originally, the fish crow was restricted to the coastal region, but it dispersed initially up the rivers, and it can be found throughout the Southeast.

Many people, including myself, have had crows as pets. Like parrots, crows can learn to imitate human speech. Their tongues do not have to be split as the myth declares. Crows are inquisitive and will gather small objects, not just shiny objects, to cache in a corner. My crow would play tug-of-war with paper or string and untie shoelaces correctly. Many studies have indicated that crows have the ability to learn "new tricks." Crows will bend straight wires into hooks to extract food from containers. Many farmers know that crows know the difference between a stick in the hand and a gun.

The boat-tailed grackle, primarily a coastal bird, could be confused with crows. Fish crows and boat-tails often feed together on the beach or marshes. The boat-tailed grackle is a member of the American blackbird family (the *Icteridae*). The European blackbird, as in the nursery rhyme "four and twenty blackbirds," is a thrush. It is all black with a yellow beak, but it sounds and behaves like our robin, "bobbing" along lawns, looking for worms.

Superficially, fish crows and grackles resemble each other and they are about the same length, though common crows are bigger. The boat-tail is more slender with a long tail. Both birds are

171

walkers. As the grackle walks, its tail moves from side to side in almost a swagger.

Additionally, crows have dark eyes, whereas grackles have yellow eyes. The female boat-tailed grackle is smaller than the male and brown. Crows wear uniform, unisex black. In bright sunlight, male grackles display shimmering hues of blue, purple, and green.

The boat-tailed grackle is a coastal bird, ranging from New Jersey to Florida and the Gulf Coast. A few move up the rivers in the Coastal Plains and an isolated population dwells in the Valdosta, Georgia, area. It is probably an extension of the Florida Gulf Coast population. The boat-tailed grackle is a social bird with unique attributes. Through much of the year, they form unisex flocks with a defined dominance hierarchy. As they are establishing their social position, males may lock their feet together and flap their wings against each other. When males have established their social position, they display to each other, beaks to heaven, often flapping their wings, creating a rattling sound. At a bird feeder, it is easy to see who is dominant.

When courting, male boat-tails spread their wings and bow to the female. Often males fly after the females over the marsh. They form harem polygamous nesting colonies, many nests in adjacent branches or trees. The females do all the work, building the nest and incubating the eggs. The dominant male perches in the center of the colony, making a lot of noisy. One or two subdominant males hang out at the edge of the colony, equally noisy. Studies of DNA have indicated that the dominant male may father most of the young and the subdominant males father a small share. The females do all the child rearing. I've observed male grackles fleeing from their begging young. Grackles' diet is thoroughly omnivorous, including palm berries, seeds, fruit, insects, small crabs, fish, dog food or cat food, and leftover human food, including potato chips and French fries. They will invade the tables on outdoor cafes, gleaning the table scraps. They will take hard food, such as dry cat food, and soak it in water before eating. Although grackles nest and roost in the trees of the maritime forest, they fish and hunt for food in the marshes and on the beach. They also nest in cattails and grasses in freshwater marshes and in cord grass in salt marches.

The common grackle resembles the boat-tailed grackle, but it is smaller and the two sexes wear the same black and glossy garb. Common throughout eastern United States, it is only an occasional visitor in the Southeast Coastal Islands. The common grackle is fairly common in the Coastal Plains, though not as abundant or obvious as the boat-tail. It nests in large communal colonies. When they visit the coastal region, they travel in groups. At birdfeeders, they defer to the larger boat-tails.

The other common blackbird in the Southeast is the red-winged blackbird. Since that bird is primarily a marsh bird. it is covered in the chapter on marshes.

The beautiful orchard oriole is a member of the blackbird family. The male is maroon and black; the female is yellow and gray. It is a fairly common summer resident throughout the Southeast. It prefers open woods or tall trees adjacent to open areas, like marshes or park-like habitats with trees. The male sings a beautiful warbling song, perched on top of a large tree such as an oak. They build a woven hanging nest; both parents brood and raise their three to five young. A pair forms a nesting territory centered around a large tree, but some orioles nest in colonies. Orioles eat insects, fruit, and nectar. Sometimes, they visit hummingbird feeders.

The brown-headed cowbirds, also a blackbird, visit the Southeast coastal region in April and May, in social flocks. After mating, the females lay their eggs in the nests of other birds, including cardinals, orioles, and warblers. When they leave, the foster parents raise the young.

Originally, an inhabitant of the plains area, the cowbirds followed the bison herds, seeking insects. With agriculture and cow farming, cowbirds spread to the East. The male is glossy black with a brown head. The female is a dull brownish-gray. It is the plainest-looking bird a birdwatcher might see.

Most tanagers, colorful birds, live in the tropics, yet a few species spend their summers in North America. The scarlet tanager (scarlet red with black wings and tail) passes through the Southeast Coast during migration, but the summer tanager breeds in the Southeast Coast. The male is our only all-red bird; the female is yellow and ochre. The summer tanager prefers mature forests, such as the Coastal Plains mixed pine-hardwood forests and open pine forest. The male sings musical, robin-like phrases, but the call notes are a series of harsh "pituiktukituk" sounds.

The yellow-billed cuckoo is fairly common in the Southeast in suitable habitats. It likes woods with thick underbrush, swamps, and riparian woods. The cuckoo is a long, lanky bird with a long tail. The whole bird is about twelve or thirteen inches long, the tail is six or seven inches. When it perches, it stretches out longitudinally rather than upright like flycatchers. The "cuc-koo" sound that we associate with clocks is the sound of the European cuckoo. The yellow-billed cuckoo makes a "squawking" noise. For this reason, it is sometimes called the "raincrow." The term "rain crow" comes from its apparent tendency to call before it is going to rain or during a rain.

Its diet is insects, especially caterpillars, and it eats bird eggs, lizards, frogs, and berries. It builds a crude nest of sticks, laying four eggs. Both sexes attend the young. Occasionally, it may adapt the habit of its European cousin, laying its eggs in other birds' nests.

The mourning dove is one of the most widespread birds in the United States, ranging from East Coast to West Coast in a variety of habitats, including open woods, forest edges, gardens, parks, agricultural lands, even deserts, but it avoids deep mature woods. The now extinct passenger pigeon, a relative of the mourning dove, was an inhabitant of the mature old- growth forests; it was a winter resident in the southeastern Coastal Plains.

The term "mourning" refers to the mournful "coo-coo" sound the dove makes. The "coo" is really a mating call. The male struts before the female with puffed-up breast, and he will nibble gently on the top of her lowered head. A courting male dove presents an engaging image of a solicitous male partner. The term "billing and cooing" is derived form the courtship behavior of doves, as is the expression "lovey dovey." They build a flimsy nest of sticks into which two eggs are laid. Both sexes care for the young, feeding them regurgitated food known as "dove milk" for the first three days.

Their food is exclusively small seeds and grain. They regularly visit bird feeders, though they usually feed on the ground, eating seeds spilled from the feeder.

One of the most rapidly proliferating doves in the Southeast is the Eurasian collared-dove. It is an introduced species that occupies much of the same habitat as the mourning dove, often feeding with them. It is a larger bird with a black collar on its neck. Its behavior is similar to the mourning dove, but its "coo" is harsher and deeper. The growing population of the collared-doves does not seem to affect the population of mourning doves.

This survey of "forest birds" ignores many species of migrants, uncommon species, and occasional visitors. Further information is available in numerous field guides to birds (see Bibliography). Birds are the most conspicuous and accessible of the wildlife of the Southeast, and the activity of "bird watching" is an engaging hobby.

I define myself as a general ecologist but I began as a bird-watcher, then extended my interest to the habitats where the birds live.

Birds

displaying male

female

Wild Turkey

Collared Dove

Mourning Doves
courting

Yellow-billed Cuckoo

Chuck-will's-widow
sitting on nest

chuck whip-poor-wil

chuck will's- wi dow

Red-bellied
Woodpecker

Downy
Woodpecker

Yellow-bellied
Sapsucker

Pileated
Woodpecker

Red-headed
Woodpecker

Flicker

Woodpeckers

Tufted Titmouse

Chickadee

tail held at angle

Carolina Wren

Brown headed Nuthatch

White-breasted Nuthatch

ruby crown

Ruby crowned Kinglet

Bluegray Gnatcatcher & nest

177

Yellow throated Warbler

Parula Warbler ♂ *female has no chest bands*

Yellow rumped Warbler *spring*

Pine Warbler

Palm Warbler *winter*

Prothonotary Warbler ♂
female is paler, olive crown

♂ ♀
Yellowthroat

Redstart ♂
female is dark gray & yellow

Warblers

Great Crested Flycatcher

Kingbird

White-eyed Vireo

Red-eyed Vireo

Cedar Waxwing

Cardinal

immature

♀

♂

♂

♀

Painted Bunting

♂

Indigo Bunting
female is brown

♀

♂

House Finch

Bluebird

♀

♂

Goldfinch

♂

Summer Tanager
female is yellow olive back

♂

Orchard Oriole
female is yellowgreen

Wood Pewee

eyering

Acadian Flycatcher

White-throated Sparrow

chestnut cap

Song Sparrow

Field Sparrow

Chipping Sparrow

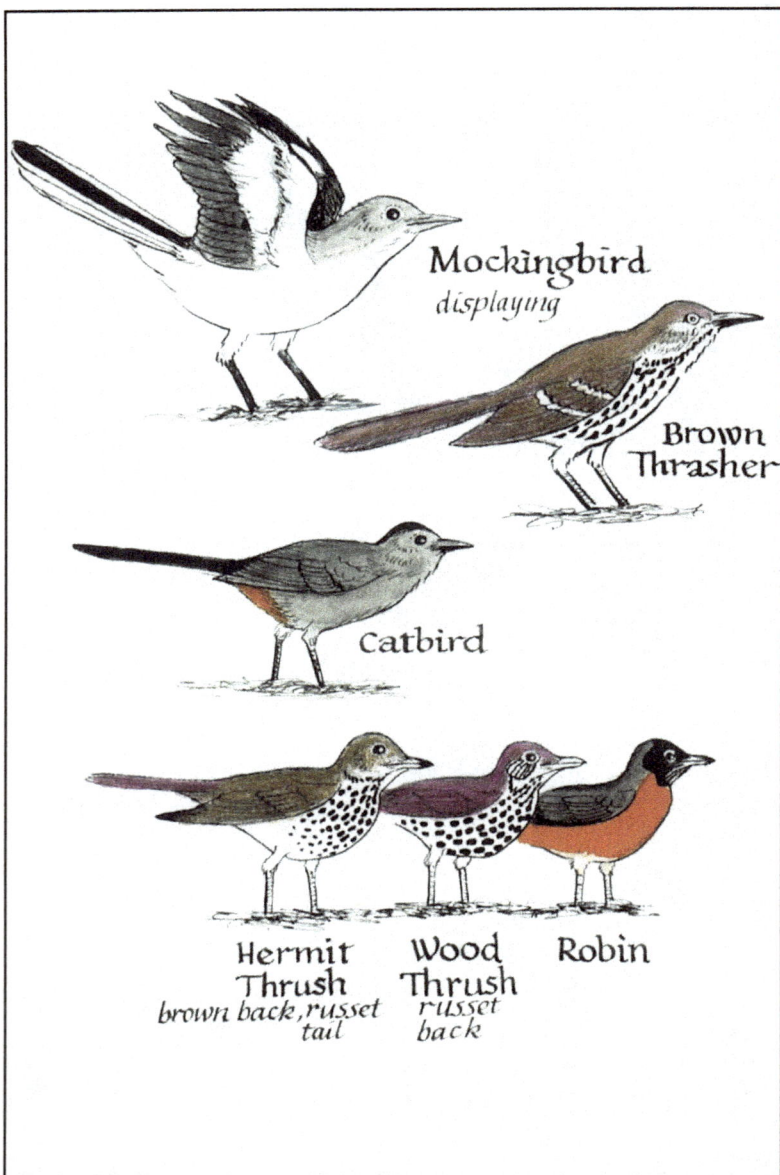

Mockingbird
displaying

Brown
Thrasher

Catbird

Hermit   Wood   Robin
Thrush   Thrush
brown back, russet   *russet*
tail   *back*

Crow

♀

yellow
eyes

Boat-tailed
Grackle

♂

displaying
Boattails

♂

Brown
headed
Cowbird

Blue
Jay

RAPTORS

Several species of raptors soar overhead, including red-tailed hawks, red-shouldered hawks, ospreys, bald eagles and vultures. Hawks and eagles usually soar alone or in pairs because they are territorial birds. A mated pair establishes a territory that it protects, especially near the nest. Vultures, on the other hand, are social and will soar and circle, as well as feed in groups. Because of their naked, rough-skinned heads, vultures are considered ugly by many people when seen close up, but they are beautiful when in flight with their broad wings stretched out and their primary feathers extended like fingers.

Vultures and many hawks are excellent soarers, making use of winds or rising hot air (thermals) to keep them aloft without the need for powered flight (wing flapping). The fingerlike, extended primary feathers help keep them aloft. The rounded wing shape of many birds works well for powered flight, but if the wing is not moving, the rounded ends produce turbulence and hence drag. The bird will then descend. The extended primary feathers of vultures and hawks have spaces between them, known as "slotting," which reduces turbulence and enables these birds to stay aloft and soar without flapping.

The two species of vultures in the Southeast are the turkey vulture, with a red head, and the black vulture, with a black head. The black vulture is the heavier of the two and has to flap regularly to keep aloft. When the two species, which often feed together, take to flight from the ground, the turkey vulture, with a few flaps, is in the air and rising, whereas the black vulture is still laboriously flapping to reach an altitude where it can soar. They are easy to distinguish when in the air. The turkey vulture has a long tail and flies with its wings held at a dihedral, like a "V," whereas the black vulture, which has a shorter tail, holds its wings flat. The black vulture also has white patches on its primary wing feathers.

Unlike hawks, which have feet with sharp claws, vultures cannot catch prey with their feet, so they eat dead animals. The black vulture, which is the more aggressive and dominant of the two, will sometimes eat live prey or begin eating before an incapacitated animal is dead. The timorous turkey vulture will not touch its prey until it is completely dead. Human beings may be repulsed by the vultures' diet, but our tastes are similar, for we, like vultures, prefer aged, tenderized meat.

Like hawks, vultures have excellent eyesight and can spot potential food from great distances. The turkey vulture also has excellent olfactory apparatus. It can smell its food. The black vultures

184

often follow turkey vultures to food sources. Vultures like to perch on high positions, including telephone poles and cell phone towers, yet they nest on the ground, often in thickets tangled in vines, hollow trees, abandoned houses, and rocky outcroppings. They have been known to regurgitate on anybody who invades their nests. In captivity, vultures can live to twenty years, though their lifespan in the wild is probably in the range of ten to fifteen years.

Many people call these birds "buzzards," but the original "buzzard" is an English and European hawk closely related to our red-tailed hawk. No vultures live in England, so the original American colonists from England applied the word "buzzard" to the soaring vultures thinking that they were related to the English buzzard. The word has persisted in American colloquial usage for vultures.

The turkey and black vultures are members of the American vulture family, which has seven species, including the world's largest flying birds, the Andean and California condors. The old-world vultures, which are found in Africa, Asia, and Southern Europe, are members of the hawk family. The American vultures had been classified as a separate family but related to hawks and old-world vultures. However, recent DNA evidence indicates that the American vultures are not related to hawks but instead are closely related to storks! This is an example of what biologists call convergent evolution where unrelated animals have evolved to resemble each other because of their lifestyle. The similar body shapes of sharks and dolphins are another example of convergent evolution. Storks are good soarers like the vultures. Some storks, like the marabou stork of Africa, are carrion eaters. The local wood stork will eat dead fish.

BUZZARDS

The red-tailed hawk, a true buzzard (Buteo), is the most common hawk throughout the United States. They build their nests atop trees. They may reuse the nests over the years, but they prefer open country with scattered trees. Sometimes, they live in urban areas, building their nests on skyscraper ledges. Although red-tails may eat birds, reptiles, including snakes, and insects, eighty-five percent of their diet is rodents. They are particularly adapted to catch rodents. The eyesight of red-tails is excellent; they can spot rats or mice in the grass from high in the air. They soar toward the prey and drop down on it. As red-tails soar overhead bright sunshine causes their spread tails to glow russet.

The red-shouldered hawk is another buzzard hawk, smaller than the red-tail but with a russet chest and shoulders. Their preferred habitats are wooded swamps and forests surrounding

185

rivers. The red-shouldered hawk eats smaller prey than the red-tails, including rats, mice, and frogs. Its feet are smaller and weaker.

In the Southeast, both of these buzzard hawks form permanent territories around the nest, guarded by the mated pair. In late summer, three or more hawks may soar together. The extra hawks are the young of that summer. By winter the young have left.

BALD EAGLE

The bald eagle is a charismatic member of the hawk family. They are in the sea eagle group (Haliaeetus) as opposed to the true eagles such as the golden eagle (Aquila). Eight species of sea eagles occur in the world, most of which have white on some part of their plumage, whether tails, heads, chests, or shoulders. The original name of our eagle was baldheaded eagle. "Bald," in this case, is an archaic word meaning white. The bald eagle is quite opportunistic in its diet. It will catch or steal fish, waterfowl, or small mammals, yet is content to eat carrion with the vultures.

In 1782, bald eagles were still common, but in the 1950s and 1960s they suffered a disastrous decline in their population. Many factors contributed to this decline, ranging from the shooting of them, since some people considered them a nuisance, to loss of habitat, and the disturbing of their nesting sites, but the major factor was the use of DDT as a pesticide. DDT accumulates in fat tissues. It becomes concentrated as it moves up the food chain with the result that the top predators have the highest concentration. A high concentration of DDT in birds results in a thinning of their eggshells. An incubating parent would crush these thin-shelled eggs. Many bird populations declined as a result of DDT, such as bald eagles, osprey, peregrine falcons, and brown pelicans. DDT was banned in the United States in 1972. Since then, bird populations are recovering. Brown pelicans and osprey are again numerous, and the bald eagle and peregrine falcon populations are increasing. When the Endangered Species Act was passed in 1973, the bald eagle was classified as an endangered species. In 1996, the United States Fish and Wildlife Service changed the status of the bald eagle from Endangered to Threatened. In 2007, the population of bald eagles had recovered sufficiently so that it was removed from the Threatened list. Bald eagles nest throughout the Southeast, but they are most abundant near the coast.

In the North, bald eagles may migrate south during cold winters; in the Southeast, these birds are permanent residents. A pair of eagles will form a permanent pair bond and establish a nesting territory. The normal life span of bald eagles is about twenty-five to thirty years. Nests are usually no closer than one mile apart. An eagle pair will defend the nest (eyrie) and its vicinity from other eagles, but the foraging range, six to fifteen miles from the eyrie, may overlap with those of neighboring eagles. In Alaska, during the salmon runs up the rivers in the spring, 2,000 to 3,000 bald eagles will gather in one place to feed.

Eagles add to their nest every year. After twenty years or so, the nest can be very large. In the North, nesting occurs in spring or early summer, in the Southeast, nesting occurs in winter. Both sexes share incubating duties.

Eagles' courtship rituals are spectacular. A pair will soar and dive together. One of the birds may flip over backwards while diving and touch or lock talons for a moment with its mate. Eagles lay two eggs, and after thirty-four to thirty-six days of incubation, the eggs hatch. In many cases, the first hatched young may dominate the second born in competing for food, resulting in the death of the second born. In three to four months, the young learn to fly (fledge) and leave the nests. During the nesting and early fledgling state, the parents are solicitous and spend much time feeding and caring for the young. Seven to eight weeks after fledging, the young, like other adolescents get restless. In addition, the adults are getting tired of taking care of them and will chase them away. The young are now on their own and have to find their food. By this time, autumn has arrived and the adults are ready to mate and raise their next brood. It takes four to five years for the young eagles to reach full maturity and find a mate. They undergo several molts, starting out as a brown bird, then brown flecked with white, then finally, the full glory of dark body with white head and tail, yellow beak and feet.

OSPREYS

The osprey has also recovered and is common wherever water is present with plenty of fish, including coastal areas, rivers, and lakes. Although they may occasionally capture birds or small mammals, the primary prey of ospreys is fish. Ospreys hover above the water when they spy a fish. Then they dive feet first, capturing the fish with their claws. The undersides of their feet have spicules that help to secure the slippery fish. Ospreys sometimes capture snakes. Then they fly to a high perch to eat the prey or take it to the nest where they tear it into chunks to feed the young.

The coastal regions of the Southeast provide perfect habitats fur the osprey: tidal waters full of fish and tall trees, like pines, perfect for nesting. Ospreys make use of lighthouses, channel markers, cell phone towers, and artificial raised platforms for nesting sites. Like eagles, ospreys add to their nests year by year, and like eagles, they are territorial. The osprey's range is worldwide. It migrates

187

south from the northern parts of its range, but along the southeastern coast (South Carolina south to Florida and the Gulf Coast), it is a permanent resident.

HARRIER

The preferred habitat of the northern harrier, sometimes called the marsh hawk, is open marsh or grasslands. It soars a few feet above the ground, wings held at a dihedral, ready to pounce on its prey, usually a small mammal, though it could be a bird, snake, or frog. The harrier has a long tail with a white rump at its base. It is found in Europe where it is known as the hen harrier. In the Southeast, this harrier is a winter resident. Curiously, only the brown females migrate to the Southeast, the gray males migrate to other regions to winter. It is not a common hawk. Only an occasional harrier can be seen soaring low over the marsh during the winter.

ACCIPTER HAWKS

Accipiter hawks are adapted for capturing birds. They are slender hawks with blunt rounded wing-tips and long tails. The buzzard hawks and harriers are adapted for soaring and dropping on their prey from above. Although Accipiters sometimes soar, they capture their bird prey by chasing them in flight, often twisting rapidly to follow their prey or to avoid branches in the forests where they may hunt. Buzzard hawks are inept at this rapid chase flight, which is why their primary prey is rodents.

Two species of Accipiters reside in the Southeast, the Cooper's hawk and the sharp-shinned hawk. The Cooper's hawk is the larger hawk (16.5 in.) and is found in the Southeast throughout the year. The smaller sharp-shinned hawk (11 in.) is a winter resident in the Southeast. The Cooper's hawk often goes after pigeons. Once I watched a Cooper's chasing a pigeon; the hawk was flying next to the pigeon, both zigzagging in rapid flight. The pigeon rolled over and escaped, the hawk shot on ahead. Often when a predator chases prey, the prey escapes. Coooper's hawks capture rodents as well as birds.

The sharp-shinned hawk ofen hides in shrubbery or the foliage until a small bird comes into view. It often hangs out near birdfeeders. It captures birds in lightning-quick surprise strikes. Because of its small size, the sharp-shiinned only goes after small birds—songbirds, small woodpeckers, or mourning doves. I once observed a sharp-shinned drop out of a tree canopy onto the ground with a cedar waxwing in its claws. Other than size, the sharp-shin can be distinguished from the Cooper's by their tails. The tip of the sharp-shinned's tail is square, whereas the tip of the Cooper's is rounded.

FALCONS AND MERLINS

Falcons are adept bird catchers. They are slender birds with pointed wings. Falcons swoop, glide, hover, dive, but only occasionally soar. The peregrine falcon's dive has been clocked at 200 miles per hour. When they hit their prey, such as a flying bird, it is either killed outright or stunned so that the falcon can grab it in its talons. The falcon's primary prey is birds, but they will eat small mammals, reptiles, or insects. Not a large bird, the peregrine is only sixteen inches long,

Although it has a worldwide distribution, in the Southeast the peregrine falcon is an uncommon winter visitor. It builds its nest on cliffs or abandoned raptor nests atop tall trees, raising three to four young. It is territorial and will defend its nest. Peregrine populations dropped because of DDT contamination, but thanks to captive breeding and reintroduction programs, the population is recovering. The most successful reintroduction programs are in large cities like New York, Chicago, and Atlanta. Peregrines nest on ledges of the tall skyscrapers, and the large population of urban pigeons provide plenty of food for the falcons.

Another uncommon winter visitor in the Southeast is the merlin, a small (ten inches) gray falcon. A bird eater, it also catches large insects like dragonflies. They frequent beaches seeking shorebirds.

The most common falcon in the Southeast is the small kestrel (nine inches). It is the most colorful hawk in the United States: russet, blue-gray with a black mask and pink breast. They can be found in the Southeast throughout the year. They build their nests in tree cavities or bird boxes. They like open country with scattered trees and perch on telephone wires. Kestrels will eat mice or lizards, but their predominant prey are insects. They hover and swoop when hunting. Their call notes are loud "killy killy killy"screams.

OWLS

Owls are a unique family of raptors, quite different from the other raptors so far described. Most owls are nocturnal and are heard more often than they are seen. They have large forward-facing eyes (binocular vision) adapted for night vision. Though their eyes are fixed and immobile, the owl can swivel its head back and forth rapidly. The ears, hidden under the feathers, are asymmetrically located on both sides of the head. This asymmetry enables the owl to locate its prey by its sounds. Additionally, the owl's stiff-feathered, facial ruff functions as a reflector, channeling sounds into the ear. The primary flight feathers have special adaptations. While the primary feathers of most birds have sharp edges, those of owls are ragged. These ragged edges muffle the sound of flight so owls can fly to their prey silently.

Great horned owls, barred owls and screech owls are forest owls widely dispersed throughout eastern United States, but they can be found in urban areas that have trees. They are permanent, non-migratory residents.

The great horned owl is our largest owl (twenty-two inches). It is a representative of a group of owls known as eagle owls (Bubo), widely dispersed throughout the world. Because of its call, this owl is called the "hooting owl." Usually solitary, but a pair will form a nesting territory to raise their young (two to three). The nest will be built in the fork of a tree, a tree cavity, cliff, cave, or sometimes on the ground, but their preference is the abandoned nest of a crow, hawk, or eagle. The great horned owl is a voracious predator, eating a variety of prey, ranging from small mammals, including skunks (the owl cannot smell), reptiles, fish, insects, and spiders, to birds including screech owls and falcons. The "horns" are tufts of feathers on both sides of the head.

The barred owl is almost as big (twenty-one inches), but it has a rounded head without any "horns." A cavity nester, it will utilize abandoned nests like the great horned owl. The barred owl has a varied diet, with its main prey being rodents and frogs. Its call, different than the "hooting owl," is a series of harsh hoots or barks rising in pitch. This owl prefers hardwood swamps.

The screech owl is a small owl (eight and a half inches) wearing either gray or russet plumage. It nests in a cavity or bird box. The screech owl's primary diet is insects, but it will eat small birds and small mammals. Its call is different from other owls: a descending, whistled whinny or a monotone trill.

The barn owl prefers open habitats including farmlands. It is a cavity nester, but it will nest in barns or other buildings. Since its primary prey are small mammals, such as rats and mice, farmers like to have them around. Its call is a hissing shriek. It has a white heart-shaped face and is sometimes called the monkey-faced owl.

This chapter describes the most commonly seen raptors in the southeast. You may observe a rare, accidental, or migrant raptor. To identify one of these uncommon sightings, check one of the standard bird field guides.

Black Vulture

wings are flat

black head

short tail

Turkey Vulture

wings at a dihedral angle

red head

long tail

Bald Eagle

immatures are brown sometimes with white flecks

Osprey

3

Northern Harrier

Eagle's nest - 1950   Spanish Hammock, Tybee GA.

Red
Shouldered
Hawk

Red-tailed
Hawk

Buteo hawks

Accipiter hawks

round tail

immature

Cooper's Hawk

square tail

Sharp-shinned Hawk

Falcons

Kestrel

Merlin

HAWKS

Peregrine Falcon

Barred owl

Great
Horned
Owl

Barn
Owl

Screech
Owl

Owls

195

SOARING BIRDS

By "soaring birds" is meant birds that spend most of their waking hours in the air, notably swifts and swallows. They catch flying insects, swallowing them in the air. Originally, swifts and swallows nested in hollow trees, grottos, or rocky cliffs, but currently they all rely on human-made structures for nesting sites.

In the primordial old-growth forests, chimney swifts nested in hollow trees, soaring high above the tree canopy, seeking out insects. Most of the virgin forests are gone, so the swifts now use chimneys as nesting sites. Historical districts like Savannah or Charleston, which have many old buildings with brick chimneys, have swarms of swifts soaring and circling above the rooftops, chattering constantly. They build a half-cup nest on the wall of the chimney or the inside of a hollow tree, gathering sticks that they glue together with their saliva. Sometimes they nest colonially.

During courtship, the swifts glide in tandem, wings held in a V-shape, They mate on the nest. Both parents incubate. The young (four or five) take to flight four weeks after hatching. They migrate south in August, returning in late March. In spring and fall, swifts roost communally.

I remember watching such a communal gathering one fall evening as the sun was setting. Thousands of swifts were swirling in a vortex above a tall industrial chimney. Gradually. they funneled into the chimney. until the last few swifts circled around and dropped into the chimney. 'By the time the chimney would be put to use to carry out smoke. the swifts would be long gone.

Swallows resemble swifts, though they are not closely related. Swifts are cousins of the night jars, whereas the swallow family is a member of the passerine or songbird group. Swifts soar high in the air, while swallows may dive down from the heights, swooping six feet or so above the ground. Swallows like open country such as marshes where they can swoop and capture insects, but they also need suitable places to nest.

Purple martins, colonial nesters, originally nested in tree cavities. At the present time, martins nest in martin houses or hanging gourds erected for them. Martins have come to depend almost entirely on human beings for nesting sites. They are common wherever nesting gourds or boxes have been installed. The martin is our largest swallow. The male is a deep blue-purple. The females and young have purple backs and gray-white under parts.

The barn swallow has the bluebird coloration of blue back and orange breast. It is a summer resident that likes to nest near open lands, such as marshes, where it can fly and feed. Originally, barn swallows nested in cliff crevices or caves. Now they nest in ledges in carports, and underneath over-hanging balconies or walls. A house with overhangs adjacent to a marsh is a perfect nest site for barn swallows; communities adjacent to marshes are perfect habitats. Old brick forts, like Fort Sumter in Charleston or Fort Pulaski in Savannah, are also good nesting sites. These forts have swarms of swallows swooping around and through them. The nest is a half-cup made of mud and straw attached to the wall. Barn swallows raise four or five young. Barn swallows may build solitary nests or they may nest in colonies. Even after the young have fledged, they and their parents return to the nest to rest or sleep.

Cliff swallows nest on bridges. Their nests, made of mud and straw, are oven-shaped with a tubular hole on the side. These swallows nest in colonies.

Purple martins, barn and cliff swallows are summer residents. The tree swallow is a winter resident in the southeastern Coastal Plains. In the north, tree swallows nest in tree cavities or bird boxes, but in the Southeast during winter, they gather in large social flocks, swirling over marshes. When insects are unavailable, tree swallows eat berries, especially the waxy bayberries. They will swirl and swarm around the bayberry shrubs (*Myrica cerifera*).

Swifts and swallows originally depended on natural places, hollow trees, cliffs, and caves, but as this region was developed, these birds adapted and now are almost entirely dependent on human-made structures for nesting sites.

HUMMINGBIRDS

During the hot summer months, people enjoy watching a tiny sprite, wings a blur, sipping nectar from a red tubular flower or a red-dyed feeder. The hummingbird is the world's smallest bird. Its behavior, metabolism, and flight patterns are different from most birds. There are 319 species of hummingbirds, all of which live in the Americas, most of them in the tropics, but we have one common species in the southeast region: the ruby-throated hummingbird. The western United States has fifteen species of hummingbirds, a few of which may show up as accidental visitors in the East. American hummingbirds are about three inches long. The smallest one is the bee hummingbird of Cuba, at one inch. The largest is the giant hummingbird of the Andes, which is eight inches.

Hummingbirds feed by sipping nectar from flowers, especially red flowers, but they readily take to feeders filled with sugar water. Hummingbirds have a high metabolism. They consume fifty percent of their weight in sugar each day. They eat small insects, which they catch in midair, and spiders. Ruby-throats also consume sap, which they obtain from holes drilled by woodpeckers. The hummingbirds were originally inhabitants of forests where they obtained nectar from forest flowers like red buckeye, trumpet flower, and begonia. They inhabit gardens, especially those with suitable flowers for feeding. Hummingbirds are strongly territorial and will aggressively defend their territory against other hummingbirds, as well as titmice, chickadees, and even blue jays.

Hummingbirds do not pair for any length of time, only making contact briefly during mating. The pair engage in vertical flight, up and down, facing each other. They copulate on the ground. Hummingbirds have tiny feet, suitable only for perching. The female builds the nest and raises the young on her own, without help from the male. She is territorial in the immediate vicinity of the nest. The tiny nest, about a half-dollar in size, is made of bud scales, plant down, and lichen, which are glued together with spider silk, built like a cup on a tree limb. The young, usually two, are born naked and are ready to fledge in about sixteen days. The young practice by whirring their wings. Finally, they lift off and hover. The young stay with their mother for about a month.

The ruby-throated hummingbird is primarily a summer resident, flying non-stop across the Gulf of Mexico to winter in Central America. A few wintering hummingbirds have been observed on the coast of Georgia.

Hummingbirds fly differently than any other birds. Terns, kingfishers, and some hawks can hover for a few moments, but hummingbirds can hover for an indefinite time as they feed. They can also fly vertically and backwards. Whereas most birds are comparable to fixed-wing airplanes, the hummingbird is comparable to a helicopter. Most birds fly with a circular motion of the wings, similar to the butterfly stroke in swimming. They do not "flap" their wings. Birds lift their wings, move them forward, bring them down, then backwards and up again, continuing in a circular motion. When the hummingbird flies, it moves its wings in an 8 pattern, reversing its wings on the backstroke so that its underside is facing upward. Large birds, like herons and pelicans, have wingstrokes of three to four beats per second. Small birds like titmice have up to twenty beats per second, but hummingbirds can fly at seventy beats per second. A hummingbird's direct flight speed can reach forty miles per hour.

Hummingbirds, distant cousins of swifts, are unique birds that are enjoyable to observe when they visit our gardens.

198

Chimney
Swift

Tree
Swallow

BarnSwallow

♂   ♀

Purple Martin

Flight
Pattern of
Swallow

Flight pattern
of Hummingbird

MAMMALS

SQUIRRELS

Most birds are diurnal and are easy to see during daylight hours. Many mammals, however, are nocturnal and secretive in behavior and are rarely seen. The exceptions are squirrels which are diurnal and may lose their fear, even begging for food in our urban parks.

Two common diurnal squirrels that live in the Southeast are the common gray squirrel (*Sciurus carolinensis*) and the larger fox squirrel (*S. niger*). The two species have different habitat requirements. The gray squirrel prefers oak-hickory forests with heavy canopies, although it is equally at home in urban parks with lots of trees. The fox squirrel prefers more open park-like forests of oak, longleaf pine, or the borders of cypress swamps.

The pelage (fur) of the gray squirrel is usually gray, but black, blonde, or white squirrels are occasionally observed. The pelage of the fox squirrel is variable, from gray to black, often with a reddish wash on the legs, sides, and tail, hence the term "fox."

Squirrels are not particularly social, but when densities are high, a dominance hierarchy is established. Dominant males will chase others through the treetops. Acorns, hickory nuts, and pine nuts are favorite foods. In addition, squirrels eat buds, fruits, and berries. Occasionally, squirrels eat animal food, such as insects, eggs, and nestlings. Squirrels will nest in tree cavities, bird boxes, or in nests made of leaves in the forks of trees.

The gray squirrel can run up to fourteen miles per hour and make leaps of four to six feet. A typical lifespan of a gray squirrel is six years, but in captivity, it can live to twelve years. The home range of a gray squirrel is between one and twenty-five acres. The fox squirrel's range averages sixty-six acres. Squirrel home ranges often overlap.

The small southern flying squirrel (*Glaucomys volans*) is abundant in the forests of the Southeast, but, because of its nocturnal habits, it escapes our notice. Unlike the other squirrels, this animal is social and will gather in tree cavity nests in groups of two to twenty-five. The "flying" squirrel does not fly but glides from tree to tree on flaps of skin stretched between their legs. Their food preferences are similar to the other species of squirrels.

RABBITS

Another commonly seen mammal is the cottontail rabbit (*Silvilagus floridanus*) which occupies diverse habitats from open woods, dunes, and upland thickets to farm lands and suburban areas. In the coastal marshes and other wet areas, especially brackish water, the cottontail is replaced by the marsh rabbit (*Silvilagus palustris*). Unlike the cottontail, the marsh rabbit is a capable swimmer. Its ears are shorter and rounder than those of the cottontail.

Cottontails are not territorial, though where their ranges overlap, they establish a "peck order." They are prolific, producing three to seven litters of three to six young each breeding season. In Georgia, each female produces fifteen to twenty-one young per year. They are the prey of predators like hawks, owls, foxes, bobcats, and coyotes, so the high productivity compensates for the high mortality especially among the young. Cottontails are most active at dusk and night. During the day, they rest in the cover of a grass tussock or a thicket of shrubs or vines. The diet of the cottontail is primarily grass and broad-leafed plants. They will eat buds, twigs, and garden plants.

MICE AND RATS

Several species of mice and rats inhabit the Coastal Plains. Although they are numerous, they are active at night and they are good hiders, so they are overlooked. Zoologists who study these animals catch them with traps.

The house mice (*Mus musculus*) and house rats that many people are familiar with are not native but were introduced from Europe and Asia. Although they may occasionally be found in field or brush, they usually stay in or near human habitation or accumulated trash, especially if there's a food source. The two species of house rats are the Norway rat (*Rattus norvegicus*) and the black rat (*Rattus rattus*). The Norway rat is the dominant species, but the black rat is the better climber. In some cases, the Norway rat may occupy the lower floors of a building, while the black rat resides in the top floors.

Peromyscus mice are the most abundant mice in the Coastal Plains. They are pretty animals with large ears and eyes and pelages that range from brown to gold. The three species of *Peromyscus* are difficult to distinguish, but they live in different habitats, although their ranges overlap. The cotton mouse (*Peromyscus gossypinus*) inhabits a variety of habitats but prefers bottomland forests and swamps; it will inhabit saw palmetto thickets. "Cotton" refers to the fact that it may use cotton to make its nest; it rarely occupies cotton fields unless they are adjacent to a swamp. The white-footed mouse (*Peromyscus leucopus*) occupies woods and brush and is widespread

201

in the Coastal Plains and throughout the East. The oldfield or beach mouse (*Peromyscus polionotus*) inhabits open sandy fields and, in some cases, beach dunes. Its color is paler than the other two species of *Peromyscus*.

The golden mouse (*Ochrotomys nuttalli*) resembles *Peromyscus* but it is less common with a spotty distribution.

Voles are also common. They are small brown mice with beady eyes and barely distinguishable ears. The meadow vole (*Microtus pennsylvanicus*), also called the meadow mouse, is abundant in meadows and grassy areas including marshes. It is common throughout the Northeast down to the Coastal Plains of the Carolinas. In Georgia, it is only common in the Piedmont. The woodland vole (*Microtus pinetarum*) is common throughout the East down to Florida, including the Coastal Plains. Its habitat ranges from woods and brush to open areas. It is most common in woods.

Most mice produce several litters per year. The voles are prolific, up to seventeen litters per year, an average of five per litter. Voles, like most mice, are vegetarian, eating grass, leaves, fruit tubers, and bark. While other species of mice will eat insects and other invertebrates, the vole appears to be a strict vegetarian.

The hispid cotton rat (*Sigmodon hispidus*) is the most abundant species of native rat in the Southeast. It is a small-eared rat, resembling a large vole. Its habitat is open fields with grass and weeds. Grass and seeds are their usual food, but they will eat agricultural crops, even eggs.

The wood rat (*Neotoma floridana*) is a beautiful animal with large eyes and ears, brown fur, and a hairy tail. It resembles a large *Peromyscus*. They have a spotty distribution in a variety of woodland habitats in the Southeast and build large nests or lodges, about three-feet wide, of sticks and leaves, which may include paper, glass, rocks, and bones. Their food is entirely vegetative: leaves, fruit, and nuts.

The marsh rice rat (*Oryzomys palustris*), an excellent swimmer, is an inhabitant of wetlands, especially the coastal salt marshes.

LARGE NOCTURNAL CREATURES

The beaver (*Castor canadensis*) is a nocturnal animal whose dams and large stick lodges may be visible. They inhabit forested areas with suitable rivers, streams, lakes, and ponds. Tree bark is a predominant diet, and they eat aquatic succulents, such as water lilies, duckweed, algae, and fleshy rootstocks. Beavers are widespread

202

throughout Georgia and the Carolinas, though they avoid marshes where alligators reside. Beavers are monogamous and produce about three to four young each spring.

The armadillo (*Dasypus novemcinctus*) is a representative of an ancient group that includes the sloths and anteaters and which has the unique attribute of its skin being covered with an armor of ossified plates. The armadillo is a digger, rooting in the earth to seek insects, millipedes, centipedes, snails, and slugs. It may eat lizards, birds' eggs, and small mammals or birds. Its gait is a shuffle; a human being can readily keep pace with one. Its range was originally Texas and south, but since the 1920s, it has been extending its range eastward and is now common in most of Georgia and Florida. The animal is common and often diurnally active on Cumberland Island National Seashore.

The opossum (*Didelphis virginiana*) is a representative of another ancient group, the marsupials, distinguished by a pouch in which they raise their young. When born, the young opossum is still virtually an embryo. It crawls into the pouch, attaches itself to a teat, and grows into a fully-formed opossum. It stays in the pouch about two months. The mother opossum's pouch accommodates six to eight young.

The habitat of the opossum is diverse, ranging from forest to agricultural lands to suburban gardens. The opossum is omnivorous, feeding on insects, earthworms, small mammals, birds, snakes, green vegetation, fruit, and berries, and carrion. They will readily eat dry dog food or cat food that is left outdoors. Opossums are solitary wanderers without territorial instincts. Nocturnal animals, they can be seen sometimes in the morning or at dusk. The opossum is unique among North American mammals in that it can hang by its tail like some South American monkeys.

RACCOONS & WEASELS

The raccoon (*Procyon lotor*) is among the most abundant of the carnivores in the United States and is found in woods, swamps, urban parks, and agricultural areas. It ranges throughout the United States to the West Coast, except for the southwestern deserts. They like to be near water, creeks, lakes, or marshes where they hunt for food like crayfish, fiddler crabs, fish, frogs, or other aquatic prey. The raccoon is omnivorous, eating both animal and vegetable food, including fruit, nuts, acorns, seeds, insects, earthworms, and small vertebrates. Raccoons are notorious for raiding bird nests for eggs. They are opportunistic and will readily consume dog food or cat

203

food, garbage, garden products, and such human junk food as potato chips and French fries. In many cases where raccoons are used to being fed, they will engage in begging activity, sometimes standing upright. A begging raccoon presents an appealing appearance, but since they are subject to rabies infection, people should exercise caution around "tame" raccoons. Raccoons are good manipulators, picking up food with both front paws and transferring it to their mouths. They will open bird feeders to obtain seed. While searching for prey in water, they will probe, grab, and knead their prey, what human beings have described as "washing their food." They have no salivary glands; hence, they must wet their food in water. They are adept climbers and excellent swimmers.

Raccoons are primarily active at night, but in locales where they are not threatened, they will be out feeding during daylight hours. The raccoon is basically a solitary animal, but if there is a good supply of food, such as at campsites, they will gather in large numbers. Females take care of their young for about five months. After that, the young forage on their own. The young remain in the den and suckle milk for the first eight to twelve weeks of their lives. Their eyes open in the third week.

Raccoons use dens for bearing the young, for winter sleep, when it is cold, and for temporary shelter. Hollow trees are their preferred dens. They may use burrows, squirrel nests, clumps of Spanish moss, dense thickets, and vacant attics, chimneys, and other human made shelters. Usually, a den is occupied by a single male or a mother with young, but up to twenty-three raccoons have been found in a single den.

Raccoons are fascinating and intelligent animals. While young, they can make good pets, but when they get old, they may become mean-tempered.

The long-tailed weasel is a small carnivore, eating small rodents and birds. It is widespread in many habitats, but it is very secretive and rarely seen. The northern long-tailed weasels turn white in the winter, when they are known as ermines, but the southern population remains brown all year.

Otters and mink, both in the weasel family, are common in the wetlands, whether fresh or salt water.

The striped skunk (*Mephitis mephitis*) is widespread in agricultural areas, grassy fields, and bushy areas throughout eastern United States. We can smell a skunk before we see it. Because of the protective effect of its effluent, the skunk is docile and often unafraid. Skunks are usually nocturnal and solitary. They make their den in burrows. Skunks are polygamous; they produce four to eight young each summer. Most predators avoid skunks unless they are under stress of extreme hunger. The great horned owl, which has no olfactory apparatus, frequently preys on skunks.

CATS & CANINES

In the past, the Southeast had two species of cats: the Florida panther (*Felis concolor coryi*) and the bobcat (*Lynx rufus*). The Florida panther, a subspecies of the cougar, once ranged from Florida throughout the Southeast up to Virginia and Kentucky. Another subspecies was found in the Northeast. About fifty or more panthers still survive in Florida, the only cougar existing in the Eastern United States. Western United States still has scattered populations of cougars, often called mountain lions. In Central and South America, this cat is called the puma.

The bobcat still survives and is widespread in the Southeast, but it is secretive and elusive. Its habitat is woods and swamps. It will live adjacent to agricultural areas provided woods, swamps, or brushy areas are available for shelter. They are a solitary animal, except for brief periods when they associate for mating. In cases where territories overlap, a dominance hierarchy is established. Two to four young are born in spring or early summer; occasionally, two litters may be produced during the summer. Bobcats' prey are rabbits, as well as squirrels, rats and mice, opossum, raccoons, fawns (rarely adult deer), birds, reptiles, insects, snails, and domestic cats. The bobcat used to be common on many of the barrier islands. It is now rare or absent on most of them. It has been reintroduced on Cumberland Island.

The red fox (*Vulpes vulpes*) and gray fox (*Urocyon cineroargenteus*) are widespread throughout eastern United States; the red fox will occupy farmlands, whereas the gray fox prefers forests and swamps. Foxes form family units, a male and female and usually three to five or more young. The usual home range is 200 to 300 acres, though it can be larger. The red fox stalks its prey like a cat. Foxes are carnivores, catching rabbits and small rodents or birds, but they will also eat fruit and nuts. The gray fox is a capable climber, unlike other canids. The red fox is reddish brown with a white tip on its tail. The gray fox has some red, but mostly it is a grizzled gray with a black tip on its tail.

In the past, the red wolf(*Canis rufus*) was the predominant wolf in the Southeast; the range of the gray wolf (*Canis lupus*) extended only to the Appalachian Mountains. The red wolf is intermediate in size between the coyote and gray wolf. Although overall a grizzled gray, it has rufous patches, which led to its name. Black is a common color variant and Bartram (in the 1700s) often observed "black wolves." It is a highly endangered canid and only survives because of a captive breeding program and reintroduction in designated locales, such as the Alligator National Wildlife Refuge on the coast of North Carolina. This population has been successful. Some red wolves have been introduced on Bull Island, South Carolina; Horn Island, Mississippi; and St. Vincent Island, Florida. As of January 1992, 151 red wolves were in existence, twenty-six in the wild (Alligator Refuge), six on captive propagation islands, and the rest in captivity. The Nashville, Tennessee and Jacksonville, Florida zoos have red wolves.

Because of hybridization with coyotes, the red wolf species was declining until the United States Fish and Wildlife Service established the captive propagation program. Many authorities believe that the red wolf is a wolf-coyote hybrid; however, ancient records, including fossil evidence, indicate that the red wolf was resident in the Southeast for a very long time.

Both species of wolves are pack animals. The pack is basically a family unit with the grown young remaining with the parents. It is a dominance hierarchy with a "top dog" (the alpha wolf) and a hierarchy of subordinates. Wolves hunt in groups; some running down the prey, while others may hide in ambush. Cats, by contrast, are solitary hunters, except for lions, sneaking up and pouncing on their prey.

Coyotes (*Canis latrans*) hunt alone or in pairs. Most of their prey is small, including mice, rabbits, and squirrels. Occasionally, they form groups to hunt larger prey such as deer. Coyotes also eat plant food, including fruit. The original range of the coyote was western United States and south through Mexico. With the elimination of wolves, coyotes have been extending their range east. Wolves will kill coyotes. All of the eastern states, including the coastal Southeast, now have coyotes.

The black bear (*Ursus americanus*) was once widespread throughout eastern United States, but in the Southeast thriving populations only exist in the forests of the Appalachian Mountains, in large swamps like the Okefenokee, and the coastal swamps and woods of North Carolina and the Florida panhandle, as well as the Everglades.

HOOFED MAMMALS

In past times, bison (*Bison bison*) and the American stag, elk, or wapiti (*Cervus elaphus*) were found in the foothills and mountains of the Southeast, but the eastern subspecies of these animals are now extinct. The white-tailed deer (*Odocoileus virginianus*) is still abundant, sometimes overabundant. Previously, populations of these deer were kept in check by cougars and wolves. Currently, the principle predator of deer is the human hunter. If the population is excessive, the understory herbs and shrubs are stripped bare by ravenous deer. The result is an undernourished, unhealthy population of deer, and many of them will die. The forest ecosystem becomes substandard affecting other animals that live there. Game managers like to maintain a deer population of seventy-five to ninety per square mile.

Although deer are basically forest animals, they do best in mixed habitat, a combination of dense cover and open areas. They do well in swamps and forest bottomlands. Deer are social animals, gathering in herds. The size of the herd depends on food sources. The herds are larger if the food is abundant. During most of the year two types of social groups form: the bucks and the does plus her offspring. Fawns may stay with their mothers for up to two years. A dominance hierarchy is established within these herds.

In the fall, when the mating begins, the social structure changes. The bucks display mating behavior over several months. These displays are known as the "rut." A dominant buck attempts to dominate up to ten does, his "harem," protecting the does from other bucks. Some clashing of antlers occurs, but rarely does the fight result in serious damage. The subdominant buck usually retreats. Young subservient bucks may be tolerated in a herd. Bucks are not sexually mature until their second year. The rut extends over several months. The antlers grow through the spring and summer months, reaching full size about August or September. At that time, the antlers harden and the buck scrapes the "velvet" skin that covered the antlers. Then the rut begins. The antlers are shed during the winter months. In general, as a buck matures, more tines are added to the antlers, up to eight tines. Other factors, such as nutrition, may affect the size of the antlers.

On the coastal islands of Georgia and South Carolina, there are smaller subspecies of white-tailed deer. The smallest is the key deer (thirty inches shoulder height) only found on Big Pine Key in southern Florida. It is an endangered species; only 250 to 300 key deer survive.

Young does of white-tailed deer give birth to one fawn in the spring, but mature does often give birth to twins. Fawns have spots which function as camouflage. When the doe is absent, the fawn lies still in the understory foliage, relying on camouflage to protect it from predators. It takes about two years for a fawn to reach maturity.

207

On some coastal islands, exotic deer have been introduced. The fallow deer, native to Europe and the Middle East, has been introduced on Little St. Simons Island on the southern Georgia coast.

One introduced exotic hoofed mammal now flourishing throughout the south is the wild hog or razorback hog (*Sus serafa*). Descended from escaped domestic pigs, after generations of breeding in the wild, they have assumed the appearance of the ancestral European wild boar. True wild boar have been introduced to crossbreed with the feral hog. In some places, notably Ossabaw Island on the coast of Georgia, the hogs have descended from pigs brought over by the Spanish in the 1600s. Hogs feed by rooting in the ground, hunting fallen acorns, nuts, or underground fungi such as truffles. They eat leaves, fruit, mushrooms, insect larvae, worms, snails, small vertebrates, and eggs. Since they can be destructive, game managers try to control their population by hunting. Hogs range through woods, bottomlands, and high marshes. They swim well and like to wallow in mud. They are common on the coastal islands. Hogs live in bands of eight or less, but the large males (boars) often wander alone.

Boars gather as females come into heat. The boars fight by slashing each other's shoulders with their tusks until a dominance hierarchy is established. The dominant boar copulates first, then rests, allowing the subordinates their turn to mate. The pregnant female goes off by herself to give birth and raise her young: one to twelve per litter with an average of seven or eight. The young are grown in one and a half years, but full maturity takes five to six years.

INSECTIVORES & BATS

The Insectivores (*Insectivora*) are small and rarely seen. The shrews are tiny at three and a half inches. Three species are in the Southeast: the southeastern shrew (*Sorex longirostris*), the short-tailed shrew (*Blarina carolinensis*), and the least shrew (*Cryptotis parva*). Shrews are ravenous carnivores, eating insects or other invertebrates, but they may attack larger animals such as mice. Because they have a high metabolism, they have to feed frequently.

Moles (*Scalopus aquaticus*) are underground mammals but the hills from their burrowing are conspicuous. The principle food of the mole is earthworms. They also eat insects, slugs, snails, centipedes, and vegetable matter. Moles will enter anthills to eat adult and larval ants. They are active at all hours throughout the year.

208

Bats are nocturnal mammals, coming out to feed at dusk. They are the only mammals that can truly fly, as opposed to flying squirrels that are gliders. The tropics, including the Florida Keys, have fruit-eating bats, but all the American species are insect eaters, catching insects on the wing. They locate their prey by echolocation, something like radar. Although bats make audible squeaks, their echolocation frequencies are higher than our audible range. These high-pitched sonar waves are bounced back by the flying insects and received by the bat's large ears. Bats have eyes, however, experimental tests have demonstrated that bats can navigate and catch their prey when their eyes are covered. Ten species of bats live in the southeastern Coastal Plain, varying in size from the small Pipistrelle (*Pipistrellus subflavus*), nine to ten inch wingspan, to the large hoary bat (*Lasiurus cinereus*) that has a wingspan of sixteen inches. The big brown bat (*Eptesicus foscus*) and red bat (*Lasiurus boreali*) are common. Their wingspans are twelve or thirteen inches. The big brown bat roosts in colonies, either in hollow trees or buildings. The red bat is a solitary, tree-roosting bat; woodlands are its preferred habitat.

Two species that have ranges in the United States limited to the southern Coastal Plains are the yellow bat (*Lasiurus intermedius*) and the Brazilian freetail bat (*Tadarida brasiliensis*). Both species range south to Central and South America. The yellow bat is uncommon and roosts in Spanish moss. The free tail bat is a colonial rooster, gathering in caves or buildings. In the Southeast, it usually inhabits cities which have attics on warehouses where they can roost.

During cold weather, many bats hibernate. In the Southeast, bats are often out flying during the warmer winter nights. Some bats migrate. Species that are only present in the Southeast during the winter months are the hoary bat and the silver-haired bat (*Lasionycteris noctivigans*).

Although the size of bats differ, most species of bats are difficult to distinguish as they fly about in the dusk. People who specialize in bats (known as Chiropterists) usually trap them in mist nets. In the hand, they can be identified. Bats carry rabies, but compared to carnivores, such as raccoons and foxes, it is rare. Less than one percent of bats carry rabies.

Bats are harmless mammals and are useful insect catchers. The nature writer, Ernest Thomson Seton, referred to them as "brownies of the air." Unfortunately, bat populations are declining, probably due to loss of habitat, including roosting sites, such as hollow trees and attics of buildings. A substitute, which is available, are bat boxes designed for bats to roost in. If more people used these bat boxes, we could restore bat populations.

This chapter is a quick survey of the southeastern mammals. For those interested in more information and detail, consult *Mammals of the Eastern United States* by John Whitaker, Jr. and William Hamilton, Jr., originally published by Cornell University Press.

Mammals

Common Mammal Tracks

Raccoon Opossum Skunk

Cottontail Armadillo

Weasel
Mink is similar

Coyote
Fox is smaller

Bobcat
no claw marks

Black Bear

White-tail Deer Hog

Squirrels

Fox Squirrel

Gray Squirrel

Flying
Squirrel

Rabbits

Marsh Rabbit

Cottontail

Cotton Rat

House Mouse

Black
Rat

Vole

Wood Rat

White-footed
Mouse

Long-tailed Weasel

Opossum

Striped Skunk

Raccoon

Beaver

Black Bear

Bobcat

Coyote

Red Wolf

Red Fox

Gray Fox

Carnivores

White-tailed Deer

Feral Hog

Florida Panther or Cougar

Nine-banded Armadillo

Common Mole

Southeastern
Shrew

Pipestrelle Bat

Hoary Bat

Big
Brown
Bat

Brazilian
Freetail Bat

IV
THE NORTH CAROLINA COAST

The coast of North Carolina is different than the coasts of South Carolina and Georgia. This coast is lined with a series of long barrier islands varying in width from about four miles to less than a mile. At the south end of the state, these islands are separated from the mainland by a narrow tidal channel, about one to four miles wide. At the north end of the state, these barrier islands, known at the Outer Banks, are separated from the mainland by Pamlico Sound (thirty miles at its widest) and the Albermarle Sound.

The natural vegetation of the islands consists of dune plants, grass meadows, brush, scrub forest, and a narrow strip of cord grass (*Spartina alterniflora*) on the leeward side. The North Carolina dunes are the site where the southern sea oats (*Uniola paniculata*) meet the northern American beach grass (*Ammophila breviligulata*). North of these islands, the dunes are covered with beach grass; sea oats cover the dunes to the south. Other dune vegetation such as panic grass (*Panicum amarum*) also grow in these dunes. Between the dunes and the salt marsh are meadows of salt meadow cord grass (*Spartina patens*). The most extensive marshes are on Pea Island National Wildlife Refuge. In addition to cord grass salt marsh, this island has freshwater cattail marshes maintained by dikes. The Pea Island marshes are excellent habitats for wading birds and wintering ducks, geese, and swans. The scrub lands are rich in yaupon holly (*Ilex vomitoria*), red bay (*Persea borbonia*), wax myrtle (*Myrica cerifera*), and Atlantic white cedar(*Chamaecyparis thyoides*). The white cedar ranges from the coasts of North Carolina to New Jersey. A few stands of this tree are found in South Carolina, but it is absent from Georgia and Florida. It grows in sandy soils near the ocean and in bogs and swamps. The islands have plenty of live oaks and loblolly pines, but palm trees are found only on the southern tip of the North Carolina coast.

Wintering geese and swans may show up anywhere in the Southeast. The largest population winter in the coastal regions of North Carolina and Virginia in saltwater and freshwater marshes. An excellent site for birdwatchers to see geese and swans is Lake Mattamuskeet National Wildlife Refuge. Lake Mattamuskeet, about five miles west of Pamlico Sound, is six miles wide and eighteen miles long but only a couple of feet in depth. The expanse of lake waters are clear of vegetation; the edges of the lake have plenty of cypress and other aquatic vegetation. At the north end of the lake is an extensive marsh area dominated by tall phragmites, invasive plants introduced from Europe where they are known as common reeds.

The lake is excellent habitat for herons, egrets, and ibis, and large numbers of wintering ducks, coots, grebes, geese, and swans. The spectacular sight is the large population of tundra swans that winter on the lake. They swim on the lake in flocks, ranging in size from a few to fifty swans. When they feed, they submerge their heads, curving their graceful necks, upending, pointing their tails to the sky as the rest of the body is submerged. Although swans will eat insects and other invertebrates, their primary diet is vegetarian. They will dig up underwater tubers with their shovel-like bills. When they lift their heads from the water, the pristine white of their head feathers are sometimes splattered with brown mud. The swans disperse to the bare, harvested agricultural fields miles from the lake to graze on the stubble left over from the harvest.

One late afternoon in December, years ago, I was standing on a levee at the north end of Lake Mattamuskeet as the swans were returning to the lake after a day of grazing in the fields. They were flying into the lake from every direction in flocks of three to forty per squadron. Sometimes. they flew in V formation, but often they flew in straggly lines. As they flew, they were "whooping." The call of the gray-headed immatures was more like a squeal. They landed with their feet stretched forward, creating a splash as their feet hit the water. The incoming swans greeted the swans that were already there by stretching out their necks. Two swans would greet each other by crossing their necks into an X pattern.

This was a spectacular sight and sound. As the swans flew over my head, I could hear the swoosh of their beating wings. and the sky echoed with the trumpeting whoops that they uttered continuously as they flew. The din from the rafting swans increased as the congregation increased. At any one moment, a hundred or more trumpeting swans would be overhead. As they would glide down to join the growing population of swimming swans, more would appear. The sky was gradually darkening, yet still they came. By this time. thousands of rafting swans were there, while more were to come.

The effect of thousands of swans whooping out of synchrony is hard to describe, but, from a distance, it is like the cacophony of whoops that come from excited fans exiting a stadium after a ball game. The chorus of a thousand swans is a continuous, throbbing sensation of high-pitched whoops. The grace of the swan has often entranced poets, including Rainer Maria Rilke and William Butler Yeats.

Canada geese also winter in North Carolina, although they are less numerous than the swans. Many of these geese now winter farther north, wherever food is available. Geese will make use of agricultural waste or scraps in urban parks. In some areas, people feed them. In many locales throughout the United States, permanent-resident, non-migratory flocks of Canada geese have become established. At least two subspecies of wintering Canada geese frequent North Carolina, one of which is conspicuously smaller. The different-sized subspecies formed flocks with their own kind. Authorities differ, but eight to ten subspecies of Canada geese have been described.

Snow geese are common on the North Carolina coast during the winter months. Two plumage types of this goose exist: the white snow goose and the blue goose, which has extensive gray areas on its body. At one time, these two types of geese were classified as separate species, but more recent evidence has demonstrated that they are color variants of the same species. The feeding habits of the snow goose are similar to those of the swans. They will graze or root in the mud for tubers or other food. The geese root in the mud like pigs, twisting their bills deep in the mud in their search for food, splattering brown on their white plumage.

The avocet (eighteen inches) is a long-legged bird with a long upturned bill. It breeds in marshes throughout the Midwest and West. Small numbers of avocets winter throughout the Southeast, but large flocks (fifty to one hundred) winter on the North Carolina Coast.

The large wintering flocks of swans and geese are spectacular sights. One of the best places to see them is the coast of North Carolina.

220

North Carolina Beaches

Atlantic White Cedar
Chamaecyparis thyoides

American Beach Grass
Ammophila breviligulata

Tundra
Swan

Canada
Goose

Snow Goose

Snow Goose
blue phase

Tundra Swans displaying

Avocet
*These birds
winter on the
North Carolina
coast.*

BIBLIOGRAPHY

GENERAL

Bartram, William. *Travels of William Bartram*, edited by Mark Van Doren. New York: Dover Publications, 1955.

Catesby, Mark. *Natural History of the Carolinas, Florida and Bahama Islands*, 1743.
MODERN EDITIONS OF THIS CLASSIC:
McBurney, Henrietta. *Mark Catesby's Natural History of America*. London: Merrell Holberton, 1997.
Feduccia, Alan. Ed. *Catesby's Birds of Colonial America*. Chapel Hill: The University of North Carolina Press, 1985.

Odum, Eugene P. *Fundamentals of Ecology*. Belmont, CA: Thomson Brooks/Cole, 2005.

Odum, W.E., E. P. Odum and H. T. Odum. "Nature's Pulsing Paradigm" in *Estuaries*, pp. 541-555, Dec. 1995.

Lippson, Robert L. and Alice Jane Lippson. *Life Along the Inner Coast*. Chapel Hill: The University of North Carolina Press, 2009.

Ray, Janisse. *Ecology of a Cracker Childhood*. Minneapolis: Milkweed Editions, 1999.

Ray, Janisse. *Pinhook*. White River Junction, VT: Chelsea Green Publishing, 2005.

Schoettle, Taylor. *A Naturalist's Guide to the Okefenokee Swamp*. Darien, GA: Darien Printing & Graphics, 2002.

Wharton C.E. *The Natural Environments of Georgia*. Atlanta: Georgia Department of Natural Resources, 1978.

BOTANY

Brown, C. L. and L. K. Kirkman. *Trees of Georgia and Adjacent States*. Portland, OR: Timber Press, 1990.

Dunbar, Lin. *Ferns of the Coastal Plain*. Columbia: University of South Carolina Press, 1989.

Duncan, W. H. and M. B. *Seaside Plants of the Gulf and Atlantic Coasts*. Washington: Smithsonian Institution Press, 1987.

Duncan W.H. and L. E. Foote. *Wildflowers of the South Eastern United States.* Athens: University of Georgia Press, 1975.

Foote L.E. and S. B. Jones. Jr. *Native Shrubs & Woody Vines of the Southeast.* Portland, OR: Timber Press, 1989.

Redford, A.E., H. E. Ahles and C. R. Bell. *Manual of the Vascular Flora of the Carolinas.* Chapel Hill: The University of North Carolina Press, 1968.

MARINE LIFE

Bachand, Robert G. *Coastal Atlantic Sea Creatures: A Natural History.* Norwalk, CT: Sea Sports Publications, 1994.

Gosner, Kenneth L. *Peterson Field Guide: A Field Guide to the Atlantic Seashore.* Boston: Houghton Mifflin, 1979

Robins, C. Richard. *Peterson Field Guide: A Field Guide to Atlantic Coast Fishes of North America.* Boston: Houghton Mifflin, 1986.

Ruppert, Edward E. and Richard Fox. *Seashore Animals of the Southeast.* Columbia: University of South Carolina Press, 1988.

Schwartz, Frank J. *Sharks, Skates and Rays of the Carolinas.* Chapel Hill: The University of North Carolina Press, 2003.

Williams, A. B. *Shrimps, Lobsters and Crabs of the Atlantic Coast of the Eastern United States, Maine to Florida.* Washington: Smithsonian Institution Press, 1984.

BIRDS

Ehrlich, P.R., D. S. Dobkin, and D. Wheye. *The Birder's Handbook: A Field Guide to the Natural History of North American Birds.* New York: Simon & Schuster, 1988.

Kaufman, Ken. *Field Guide to the Birds of North America.* Boston: Houghton Mifflin, 2000.

Peterson, Roger Tory. *Field Guide to the Birds of Eastern and Central North America.* Boston: Houghton Mifflin, 2010.

Sibley, David Allen. *Field Guide to the Birds of Eastern North America.* New York: Alfred A Knopf, 2003.

Schneider, T. M., Ed. *The Breeding Bird Atlas of Georgia.* Athens: University of Georgia Press, 2010.

MAMMALS

Bowers, Nora, Ken Kaufman and Rick Bowers. Kaufman *Field Guide to the Mammals of North America*. Boston: Houghton Mifflin, 2004.

Burt, W. H., R. T. Peterson and R. P. Grossenheider . *Peterson Field Guide: Field Guide to Mammals: North America north of Mexico*. Boston: Houghton Mifflin, 1980.

Whitaker, John O., Jr. and Williams J. Hamilton, Jr. *Mammals of the Eastern United States*. Ithaca, NY: Comstock Pub. Associates, 1998.

Whitaker John O, Jr. *National Audubon Society Guide to North American Mammals*. New York: Knopf, distributed by Random House, 1996.

REPTILES AND AMPHIBIANS

Conant, Roger, and Joseph Collins. *Peterson Field Guide: Reptiles and Amphibians: eastern and central North America*. Boston: Houghton Mifflin, 1998..

Jensen, John et al. *Amphibians and Reptiles of Georgia*. Athens: University of Georgia Press, 2008.

228

229

231

MAUDLIN POND PRESS
maudlinpond.com

MAUDLIN POND PRESS was founded in the throes of the 2020 COVID-19 pandemic by a group of authors on Tybee Island. Their partnership was intended to provide a platform to make publishing easier than the pure self-publishing experience for new authors. With the goal of publishing new literary works by established and new authors, the company obtains literary works, determines the feasibility of publishing those works, preparing the for publication, including editing, formatting, arranging artwork when need, obtaining copyrights, and then marketing those books as online and in-print publications.

Maudlin Pond Press
PO Box 53
Tybee Island, GA 31328
Phone: +1 (912) 433-1158
https://maudlinpond.com/

www.ingramcontent.com/pod-product-compliance
Lightning Source LLC
Chambersburg PA
CBHW072104040426
42334CB00042B/2326